The

AUSTRIAN
Theory *of the*
Trade Cycle
and other essays

Ludwig von Mises
Gottfried Haberler
Murray N. Rothbard
Friedrich A. Hayek

Compiled by Richard M. Ebeling
With an Introduction and Summary by Roger W. Garrison

MISES
INSTITUTE

518 West Magnolia Avenue
Auburn, Alabama 36832-4528
www.mises.org

Ludwig von Mises

Gottfried Haberler

Friedrich A. Hayek

Murray N. Rothbard

Dedicated to the memory of O. P. Alford, III,
champion of liberty and the Austrian School

Published by the Ludwig von Mises Institute, Auburn, Alabama
36832-4528.

Library of Congress Catalog Card Number 96-075695.

ISBN: 0-945466-21-8

Contents

Introduction: The Austrian Theory in Perspective
Roger W. Garrison 7

The "Austrian" Theory of the Trade Cycle
Ludwig von Mises 25

Money and the Business Cycle
Gottfried Haberler 37

Economic Depressions: Their Cause and Cure
Murray N. Rothbard 65

Can We Still Avoid Inflation?
Friedrich A. Hayek 93

The Austrian Theory: A Summary
Roger W. Garrison 111

Index 123

About the Authors 127

Introduction:
The Austrian Theory
in Perspective

Roger W. Garrison

The four essays in this volume, each written by a major figure in the Austrian school of economics, set out and apply a distinctive theory of the business cycle. The span of years (1932–1970) over which they appeared saw a dramatic waxing and then waning of the prominence—both inside and outside the economics profession—of the Austrian theory. Gottfried Haberler wrote in his 1932 essay that the theory "is not so well known in this country as it deserves to be" (pp. 44). Although Ludwig von Mises offered no assessment in this regard in his essay, he remarked in 1943 about the effect of the theory's general acceptance on the actual course of the cycle. Anticipating a key insight in the modern literature on "rational expectations," Mises wrote, "The teachings of the monetary theory of the trade cycle are today so well known even outside the circle of economists that the naive optimism which inspired the entrepreneurs in the boom periods has given way to greater skepticism."[1] Then, in 1969, Murray N. Rothbard could write—without serious overstatement—that "a correct theory of depressions and of the business cycle *does* exist, even though it is universally neglected in present-day economics" (p. 74).

What happened over the span of nearly forty years to account for the rise and fall of this theory of boom and bust? The simple answer, of course, is: the Keynesian revolution. John Maynard Keynes's *General Theory of Employment, Interest, and Money*, which made its appearance in 1936, produced a major change in the way that economists deal with macroeconomic issues. A close look at some pre-Keynesian ideas can show why the Austrian theory was so easily lost in the aftermath of the Keynesian revolution; a brief survey of the alternatives offered by modern macroeconomics will show why there is a new-found interest in this old Austrian theory.

First introduced by Mises in his *Theory of Money and Credit* (1912), the theory was originally billed as the circulation credit theory rather than as a uniquely Austrian theory. Mises was very much aware of its multinational roots. The notion that the market process can be systematically affected by a divergence between the bank rate of interest and the natural rate came from Swedish economist Knut Wicksell; the understanding

---

[1]Ludwig von Mises, "Elastic Expectations and the Austrian Theory of the Trade Cycle," *Economica*, ns. 10 (August 1943): 251.

that the process so affected would have a self-reversing quality to it (Mises used the term "counter-movements" in his earliest exposition) came from the British currency school, whose analysis featured international gold flows. The uniquely Austrian element in Mises's formulation is the capital theory introduced by Carl Menger and developed by Eugen von Böhm-Bawerk. Mises showed that an artificially low rate of interest, maintained by credit expansion, misallocates capital, making the production process too time-consuming in relation to the temporal pattern of consumer demand. As time eventually reveals the discrepancy, markets for both capital goods and consumer goods react to undo the misallocation. The initial misallocation and eventual reallocation constitute the microeconomic foundations that underlie the observed macroeconomic phenomenon of boom and bust. Mises's theory was superior to its Swedish forerunner in that Wicksell was concerned almost exclusively with the effect of credit expansion on the general level of prices. It was superior to its British forerunner in that the currency school's theory applied only when monetary expansion in one country outpaced that of its trading partners. Mises's theory was applicable even to a closed economy and to a world economy in which all countries are experiencing a credit expansion.

The theory took on a more predominantly Austrian character in the hands of F. A. Hayek. In the late 1920s and early 1930s, Hayek gave emphasis to the Austrian vision of capital that underlies the business cycle theory by introducing a simple graphical representation of the structure of production. He used right triangles that change in shape to illustrate a change in the economy's capital structure.[2] Hayek focused the analysis clearly on the relationship between the roundaboutness of the production process and the value of the corresponding output. The Hayekian triangles keep track of both time and money as goods-in-process make their way through the temporally sequenced stages of production. His notion of a linear production process is highly abstract and overly simple in the light of a fuller accounting of the fixed and circulating capital that actually characterize a capital-using economy. However, these triangles feature an essential but often neglected dimension—the time dimension—in the account of boom and bust. Alternative theories, in which consumption and investment appear as two coexisting aggregates, can be seen as even more simplistic—to the point of being wholly inadequate for analyzing the boom-bust sequence.

Haberler concludes his essay with an expression of concern about the complexity of the Austrian theory, which he saw as a "serious disadvantage" (p. 64). But the complexity, in his judgment, is inherent in the subject matter and hence is not a fault of the theory. Complexity is evident in the two early essays (1936 and 1932) in their organization and style

[2]Friedrich A. Hayek, *Prices and Production*, 2nd ed. (New York: Augustus M. Kelley, 1935).

of argument. Both Mises and Haberler defend the theory against its critics and deal with various misunderstandings. Mises, for instance, identifies Irving Fisher's inflation premium, which attaches itself to the rate of interest as prices in general rise, only to say that this is *not* what he is talking about. He is discussing, instead, still another aspect of interest-rate dynamics. The *real* rate of interest rises at the end of the boom to reflect the increasing scarcity of circulating capital, after excessive amounts of capital have been committed to the early stages of production processes (p. 31). Haberler takes great pains to refocus the reader's attention away from the general price level and toward the relative prices that govern the "vertical structure of production" (p. 49). He distinguishes between "absolute deflation" and "relative deflation," and between "primary and fundamental" phenomena that characterize the downturn and "secondary and accidental" phenomena that may also be observed. All these complexities—plus still others involving such notions as the natural rate of interest and the corresponding degree of roundaboutness of the production process—are unavoidable in a theory that features an intertemporal capital structure. The theoretical richness that stems from the attention to capital has as its negative counterpart the expositional difficulties and scope for misunderstanding.

Keynes offered the profession relief from all this by articulating—though cryptically—a capital-free macroeconomics. As Rothbard's discussion implies, all the thorny issues of capital theory were simply swept aside. An alternative theory that featured the playoff between incomes and expenditures left little or no room for a capital structure. Investment was given special treatment not because of its link to future consumption but because spending on investment goods is particularly unstable. Uncertainties, which are perceived to be a deep-seated feature of market economies, dominate decision making in the business community and give play to psychological explanations of prosperity and depression. And the notion that depression may be attributable to pessimism on the part of the business community suggests a need for central direction and policy activism. Prosperity seems to depend upon strong and optimistic leadership in the political arena. Relief from the complexities of capital theory together with policy implications that were exceedingly attractive to elected officials gave Keynesianism an advantage over Austrianism. An easy-to-follow recipe for managing the macroeconomy won out over a difficult-to-follow theory that explains why such management is counterproductive.

Tellingly, the two later essays (1969 and 1970) are as much about Keynesianism as about Austrianism. Rothbard and Hayek are trying anew to call attention to a theory that had been buried for decades under the Keynesian avalanche. Rothbard deals with the Phillips curve, which purports to offer a choice to political leaders between inflation and unemployment; Hayek deals with the wage-price spiral, which had captured the attention of journalists and textbook authors for much of the postwar era. The need for dealing critically with Keynesianism—and with monetarism—while at the same time reintroducing the key considerations from capital theory meant that the Austrian theory of the business cycle was an even harder sell in the 1970s than it had been a half-century earlier.

The offering of these four separate and distinct essays on the Austrian theory carries the message that there is no single canonical version of the theory. Our understanding of boom and bust is not based upon some pat story to be told once and for all time. Rather, the theory allows for variations on a theme. The market works; it tailors production decisions to consumption preferences. But production takes time, and as the economy becomes more capital intensive, the time element takes on greater significance. The role of the interest rate in allocating resources over time becomes an increasingly critical one. Still, if the interest rate is right, that is, if the interplay between lenders and borrowers is allowed to establish the natural rate, then the market works right. However, if the interest rate is wrong, possibly because of central bank policies aimed at "growing the economy," then the market goes wrong. The particulars of just how it goes wrong, just when the misallocations are eventually detected, and just what complications the subsequent reallocation might entail are all dependent on the underlying institutional arrangements and on the particular actions of policy makers and reactions of market participants.

The essays leave much scope for solving puzzles, for refining both theory and exposition, and for applying the theory in different institutional and political environments. One enduring puzzle emerges from the writings of several economists, including Haberler, who once embraced the theory enthusiastically but subsequently rejected it. The key question underlying the recantations is easily stated: Can the intertemporal misallocation of capital that occurs during the boom account for the length and depth of the depression? Haberler provides one of the best answers to this question—one that is most favorable to the Austrian theory—in his 1932 essay. The "maladjustment of the vertical structure of production," to use Haberler's own term, does not, by itself, account for the length and depth of the depression. Rather, this policy-induced change in the intertemporal structure of capital is the basis for the claim that a crisis and downturn are inevitable. The reallocation of resources that follows the downturn, which largely mirrors—both qualitatively and quantitatively—the earlier misallocation, involves an abnormally high level of (structural) unemployment but need not involve a deep and lengthy depression.

However, complications that may well accompany the market's adjustment to a policy-induced intertemporal misallocation can cause the depression to be much deeper and longer than it otherwise would be. The same policy makers who orchestrated the artificial boom may well behave ineptly when they see that the ultimate consequence of their policy is a bust. Their failure to stem the monetary contraction together with interventions by the legislature that prop up prices and wages and strengthen trade barriers will make a bad situation worse. All such complications, which play themselves out as a self-aggravating contraction, are correctly identified by Haberler as "secondary phenomena." This term is not employed to suggest that these aspects of the depression are negligible or second-order in importance. "[I]t may very well be," Haberler explains, "that this secondary wave of depression, which is induced by the more fundamental maladjustment, will grow to an overwhelming importance" (p. 58). Though possibly overwhelming, the effects of the complications are still secondary in the sense of temporal and causal ordering.

The puzzle in all this emerges when we read Haberler's 1976 recantation of the Austrian theory, which echoed Lionel Robbins's heartfelt recantation of a few years earlier. Mises refers to Robbins's 1934 book, *The Great Depression*, as "the best analysis of the actual crisis" (p. 28 n). In 1971 Robbins wrote in his autobiography that this is a book "which [he] would willingly see forgotten."[3] Drawing on Robbins's recantation,

---

[3] Lionel Robbins, *An Autobiography of an Economist* (London: Macmillan, 1971), p. 154.

Haberler offers the opinion that the "real maladjustments, whatever their nature, 'were completely swamped by vast deflationary forces.'" But rather than suggest, as he had earlier, that these forces could easily have been "induced by the more fundamental maladjustments," he simply attributes them to "institutional weaknesses and policy mistakes."[4] The astute reader will see Haberler's 1932 discussion of secondary phenomena as an insightful and hard-hitting critique of the 1976 Haberler—and would see a similar relationship between the 1934 Robbins and the 1971 Robbins.

In 1932, Haberler alluded to the "economic earthquakes" (p. 37) that Western countries had experienced. He might have put the earthquake metaphor to further use in accounting for the relationship between primary and secondary issues. During the 1906 earthquake in San Francisco, for instance, fires broke out and caused much more destruction than had been caused by the actual quaking of the earth. Even so, the fire was a secondary phenomenon; the quake was the primary phenomenon. The fact that the length and depth of the Great Depression are to be accounted for largely in terms of secondary phenomena, then, does not weigh against our understanding that the primary phenomenon was the quaking

---

[4]Gottfried Haberler, *The World Economy, Money, and the Great Depression 1919–1939* (Washington, D.C.: American Enterprise Institute, 1976), p. 26. Also, see Haberler, "Reflections on Hayek's Business Cycle Theory," *Cato Journal* 6, no. 2 (Fall 1986): 421–35.

of the capital structure. What accounts, then, for the recantation of these Austrian theorists—and of several others, including John R. Hicks, Nicholas Kaldor, and Abba P. Lerner? This puzzle remains to be solved.

Expositional difficulties derive largely from the fact that the capital-based macroeconomics of the Austrian school and particularly the Austrian theory of the business cycle are foreign to modern economists whose training is exclusively in labor-based macroeconomics. In today's profession, a given capital stock has become one of the defining assumptions underlying the conventional macroeconomic relationships. To allow capital to be a variable rather than a parameter is to change the subject matter—from macroeconomics to the economics of growth. Further, modern economists tend to think of capital holistically in terms of stocks and flows, which precludes any consideration of changes—to say nothing of unsustainable changes—in the capital structure. Gordon Tullock's bafflement at the Austrian theory is illuminating in this regard. Tullock takes Rothbard's essay as canonical and explains "Why the Austrians Are Wrong about Depressions." This article, together with a comment by Joseph T. Salerno and reply by Tullock, merit careful study.[5] According to Tullock's understanding of the Austrian theory, the boom is a period during which the flow of consumer goods is sacrificed

---

[5] Gordon Tullock, "Why the Austrians Are Wrong about Depressions," *Review of Austrian Economics* 2 (1987): 73–78; Joseph T. Salerno, "Comment on 'Why the Austrians

so that the capital stock can be enlarged. At the end of the boom, then, the capital stock would actually be larger, and the subsequent flow of consumer goods would be correspondingly greater. Therefore, the period identified by the Austrians as a depression would, instead, be a period marked by increased employment (labor is complementary to capital) and a higher standard of living. The stock-flow construction that underlies this line of reasoning does not allow for the structural unemployment that characterizes the crisis—much less for the complications in the form of the secondary depression.[6] This exchange between Tullock and Salerno gives the modern student of Austrianism a good feel for the challenge involved in the exposition of Austrian theory in an academic environment unreceptive to a capital-based macroeconomics.

Capital-based macroeconomics is simply macroeconomics that incorporates the time element into the basic construction of the theory. Investment now is aimed at consumption later. The interval of time that separates this

---

Are Wrong about Depressions,'" *Review of Austrian Economics* 3 (1989): 141–45; and Tullock, "Reply to Comment by Joseph T. Salerno," idem.: 147–49.

[6]Tullock on the basis of a peculiar judgment about the relative size of the economy's producer goods sector, makes a minor concession to the Austrian theory: It applies to "those factories and machine tools that were less than 40 percent completed [at the end of the boom]." But, "the producer goods industries are always a fairly small part of the economy. In that small part, however, undeniably a Rothbard, Austrian type of depression would cause a cutback in production and laying off of personnel."

employment of means and the eventual achievement of ends is as fundamental a variable as are the more conventional ones of land and labor. The Austrian theory features the time element by showing what happens when the economy's production time, the degree of roundaboutness, is thrown out of equilibrium by policies that override the market process. Beyond this general understanding, as already suggested, the focus of particular expositions vary in accordance with the historical and institutional setting. The fact that each of the essays in this volume reflects its own time and setting does not imply a myopia on the part of its author. Rather, it suggests the versatility of the theory.

Writing in the early 1930s, for instance, Mises called attention to the "flight into real values" (p. 30) that characterizes a hyperinflation, such as the one experienced in Germany in 1923. The lesson, though, transcends the insights into that particular historical experience. If, over a period of years, capital has been misallocated by an accelerating credit expansion, there is no policy that avoids a crisis. In the modern vernacular, there is no possibility of a "soft landing."[7] Decelerating the expansion will cause real interest rates to rise dramatically as credit becomes increasingly scarce; bankruptcies would follow. Further accelerating the

---

[7]This is not to deny the difference between a hard landing with no complications and a crash, in which the complications dominate.

expansion will cause hyperinflation and a collapse of the monetary system. Mises is telling us, in effect, that the central bank can print itself into trouble, but it cannot print itself out of trouble. Writing in 1970, Hayek refers to the central bank's dilemma by suggesting that on the eve of the crisis the policy makers find themselves "holding a tiger by the tail." He gives play to the political and economic forces that were then dominant by relating them to the commonly perceived wage-price spiral that accompanies a prolonged expansion. The final throes of the boom take the form of a duel between labor unions, which have the political power to force wage rates higher, and the central bank, which can bring them back down (in real terms) by accelerating the rate of inflation. Although Hayek, above all others, is to be credited with shifting the focus of business cycle theory from labor markets to capital markets, he offers few clues in this essay about disequilibrium in the intertemporal structure of production. Instead, he recognizes that the political and economic dynamics of the period have given special relevance to the problem—he even calls it the "central problem" (p. 110)—of wage determination.

The application of the Austrian theory of the business cycle in today's economy would give little play to the fear of hyperinflation or to the problem of a wage-price spiral. The central problem today is chronic and dramatic fiscal imbalance. Budget deficits rather than credit expansion are bound to be the focus in any plausible account of the effect of the government's macroeconomic policy on the economy's performance. Still, the central bank figures importantly into the story. The very *potential* for monetizing the Treasury's debt eliminates the risk of default, and thereby puts the Treasury on a much longer leash than it would otherwise enjoy. The problem of an artificially low rate of interest in earlier episodes is overshadowed by the problem of an artificially low risk premium on government debt. Although risk-free to the holders of Treasury securities, this black cloud of debt overhangs the market for private securities, distorting the economy's capital structure and degrading its performance generally. There are some modern applications of the Austrian theory that take these considerations into account, but much remains to be done.[8]

A stocktaking of the modern alternatives to the Austrian theory suggests that capital-based macroeconomics may be due for a comeback. Conventional Keynesianism, whether in the guise of the principles-level Keynesian cross, the intermediate IS-LM, or the advanced AS/AD is formulated at a level of aggregation too high to bring the cyclical quality of boom and bust into full view. Worse, the development of these tools of analysis in the hands of the modern textbook industry has involved a serious sacrifice of substance in favor of pedagogy.

[8]Roger W. Garrison, "Hayekian Triangles and Beyond," in Jack Birner and Rudy van Zijp, eds., *Hayek, Coordination and Evolution* (London: Routledge, 1994), pp. 109–25; and Roger W. Garrison, "The Federal Reserve Then and Now," *Review of Austrian Economics* 8, no. 1 (1994): 3–19.

Students are taught about the supply and demand curves that represent the market for a particular good or service, such as hamburgers or haircuts. Then they are led into the macroeconomic issues by the application of similar-looking supply and demand curves to the economy as a whole. The transition to aggregate supply and aggregate demand, which is made to look deceptively simple, hides all the fundamental differences between microeconomic issues and macroeconomic issues. While these macroeconomic aggregates continue to be presented to college undergraduates, they have fallen into disrepute outside the classroom. One recent reconsideration of the macroeconomic stories told to students identifies fundamental inconsistencies in AS/AD analysis.[9]

Conventional monetarism employs a level of aggregation as high as, if not higher than, that employed by Keynesianism. While Milton Friedman is to be credited with having persuaded the economics profession—and much of the general citizenry—of the strong relationship between the supply of money and the general level of prices, his monetarism adds little to our understanding of the relationship between boom and bust. The monetarists have effectively countered the Keynesians on many fronts, but they share with them the belief that macroeconomics and even business cycle theory

---

[9]David Colander, "The Stories We Tell: A Reconsideration of AS/AD Analysis," *Journal of Economic Perspectives* 9, no. 3 (Summer 1995): 169–88.

can safely ignore all considerations of a capital structure. Modern spin-offs of monetarism, which incorporate the ideas of rational expectations and instantaneous market clearing, have brought the time element back into play. Overlapping-generations models and particularly the time-to-build models seem to have some relationship to Austrian ideas. But the emphasis on the development of modeling techniques over the application of the theory to actual episodes of boom and bust has greatly diminished the relevance of this strand of macroeconomic thought.[10]

In recent years, there has been an increasingly widespread recognition that modern macroeconomics is in disarray. Today's textbooks and professional journals are replete with models that, while impressive in their display of technique, are profoundly implausible and wholly inapplicable to the world as we know it. The inadequacies of modern macroeconomics have caused some academicians to wonder (if only facetiously): How far back do we have to go before we can start all over? The essays in this volume provide a substantive answer to that question. We have to go back about sixty years to a time when capital theory was an integral part of macroeconomics.

---

[10]On the relationship between new classical theory and Austrian theory, see Kevin Hoover, "An Austrian Revival?" in Hoover, *The New Classical Macroeconomics: A Skeptical Inquiry* (Cambridge: Basil Blackwell, 1988), pp. 231–57; and Roger W. Garrison, "New Classical and Old Austrian Economics: Equilibrium Business Cycle Theory in Perspective," *Review of Austrian Economics* 5, no. 1 (1991): 91–103.

We have to go back to the Austrian school. A modernized capital-based macroeconomics can compare favorably with any of the present-day rivals.

Murray Rothbard's essay ends with an anticipation of the Austrian revival—which actually began, with his help, in 1974. This volume is offered in the spirit of Rothbard and in the hope that the Austrians will have an increasing influence in the years ahead on the development of business cycle theory.

THE "AUSTRIAN" THEORY
OF THE TRADE CYCLE

Ludwig von Mises

Nowadays it is usual in economics to talk about the Austrian theory of the trade cycle. This description is extremely flattering for us Austrian economists, and we greatly appreciate the honor thereby given us. Like all other scientific contributions, however, the modern theory of economic crises is not the work of one nation. As with the other elements of our present economic knowledge, this approach is the result of the mutual collaboration of the economists of all countries.

The monetary explanation of the trade cycle is not entirely new. The English "Currency School" has already tried to explain the boom by the extension of credit resulting from the issue of bank notes without metallic backing. Nevertheless, this school did not see that bank accounts which could

This essay was originally published as "La Theorie dite Autrichienne de Cycle Économique," in the *Bulletin* of the Sociéte Belge d'Etudes et d'Expansion (1936): 459–64. It was translated from the French by David O'Mahoney and J. Huston McCulloch.

be drawn upon at any time by means of checks, that is to say, current accounts, play exactly the same role in the extension of credit as bank notes. Consequently the expansion of credit can result not only from the excessive issue of bank notes but also from the opening of excessive current accounts. It is because it misunderstood this truth that the Currency School believed that it would suffice, in order to prevent the recurrence of economic crises, to enact legislation restricting the issue of bank notes without metallic backing, while leaving the expansion of credit by means of current accounts unregulated. Peel's Bank Act of 1844, and similar laws in other countries, did not accomplish their intended effect. From this it was wrongly concluded that the English School's attempt to explain the trade cycle in monetary terms had been refuted by the facts.

The Currency School's second defect is that its analysis of the credit expansion mechanism and the resulting crisis was restricted to the case where credit is expanded in only one country while the banking policy of all the others remains conservative. The reaction which is produced in this case results from foreign trade effects. The internal rise in prices encourages imports and paralyses exports. Metallic money drains away to foreign countries. As a result the banks face increased demands for repayment of the instruments they have put into circulation (such as unbacked notes and current accounts), until such time as they find they have to restrict credit. Ultimately the outflow of specie checks the rise in prices. The Currency School analyzed only this particular case; it did not consider credit expansion on an international scale by all the capitalist countries simultaneously.

In the second half of the 19th century, this theory of the trade cycle fell into discredit, and the notion that the trade cycle had nothing to do with money and credit gained acceptance. The attempt of Wicksell (1898)[1] to rehabilitate the Currency School was short-lived.

The founders of the Austrian School of Economics—Carl Menger, Böhm-Bawerk, and Wieser—were not interested in the problem of the trade cycle. The analysis of this problem was to be the task of the second generation of Austrian economists.[2]

---

[1]Knut Wicksell, *Interest and Prices*, R. F. Kahn, trans. (New York: Augustus M. Kelley, 1965)—Tr.

[2]The principal Austrian works concerning the theory of the economic cycle [as of 1936] are: Mises, *The Theory of Money and Credit* (New York: Foundation for Economic Education, 1971; translation of the 2nd German edition, 1924; originally published in 1912); Mises, *Monetary Stabilization and Cyclical Policy* (1928) reprinted in *On the Manipulation of Money and Credit*, Percy L. Greaves, ed., Bettina Bien Greaves, trans. (Dobbs Ferry, N.Y.: Free Market Books, 1978; originally published as a monograph in German); Friedrich A. von Hayek, *Monetary Theory and the Trade Cycle* (New York: Augustus M. Kelley, 1966; reprint of 1933 English edition, originally published in German in 1929); Hayek, *Prices and Production* (New York: Augustus M. Kelley, 1967; reprint of 1935 2nd revised edition, originally published in 1931); Fritz Machlup, *Führer durch die Krisenpolitik* (1934); Richard von Strigl, *Capital and Production*, Margaret Rudelich Hoppe and Hans-Hermann Hoppe, trans. (Auburn, Ala.: Ludwig von Mises Institute, 1995; translation of

In issuing fiduciary media, by which I mean bank notes without gold backing or current accounts which are not entirely backed by gold reserves, the banks are in a position to expand credit considerably. The creation of these additional fiduciary media permits them to extend credit well beyond the limit set by their own assets and by the funds entrusted to them by their clients. They intervene on the market in this case as "suppliers" of additional credit, created by themselves, and they thus produce a lowering of the rate of interest, which falls below the level at which it would have been without their intervention. The lowering of the rate of interest stimulates economic activity. Projects which would not have been thought "profitable" if the rate of interest had not been influenced by the manipulations of the banks, and which, therefore, would not have been undertaken, are nevertheless found "profitable" and can be initiated. The more active state of business leads to increased demand for production materials and for labor. The prices of the means of production and the wages of labor rise, and the increase in wages leads, in turn, to an increase in prices of consumption goods. If the banks were to refrain from any further extension of credit and limited themselves to what they had already done, the boom would rapidly halt. But the banks do not deflect from their

---

edition); the best analysis of the actual crisis was made by Sir Lionel Robbins, *The Great Depression* (Freeport, R.I.: Books for Libraries Press, 1971; reprint of 1934 edition).—[Note: citations have been updated in this new edition.]

course of action; they continue to expand credit on a larger and larger scale, and prices and wages correspondingly continue to rise.

This upward movement could not, however, continue indefinitely. The material means of production and the labor available have not increased; all that has increased is the quantity of the fiduciary media which can play the same role as money in the circulation of goods. The means of production and labor which have been diverted to the new enterprises have had to be taken away from other enterprises. Society is not sufficiently rich to permit the creation of new enterprises without taking anything away from other enterprises. As long as the expansion of credit is continued this will not be noticed, but this extension cannot be pushed indefinitely. For if an attempt were made to prevent the sudden halt of the upward movement (and the collapse of prices which would result) by creating more and more credit, a continuous and even more rapid increase of prices would result. But the inflation and the boom can continue smoothly only as long as the public thinks that the upward movement of prices will stop in the near future. As soon as public opinion becomes aware that there is no reason to expect an end to the inflation, and that prices will continue to rise, panic sets in. No one wants to keep his money, because its possession implies greater and greater losses from one day to the next; everyone rushes to exchange money for goods, people buy things they have no considerable use for without even considering the price, just in order to get rid of the money. Such is the phenomenon that occurred in Germany and in other countries that followed a policy of prolonged inflation and that was known as the "flight into real values." Commodity prices rise enormously as do foreign exchange rates, while the price of the domestic money falls almost to zero. The value of the currency collapses, as was the case in Germany in 1923.

If, on the contrary, the banks decided to halt the expansion of credit in time to prevent the collapse of the currency and if a brake is thus put on the boom, it will quickly be seen that the false impression of "profitability" created by the credit expansion has led to unjustified investments. Many enterprises or business endeavors which had been launched thanks to the artificial lowering of the interest rate, and which had been sustained thanks to the equally artificial increase of prices, no longer appear profitable. Some enterprises cut back their scale of operation, others close down or fail. Prices collapse; crisis and depression follow the boom. The crisis and the ensuing period of depression are the culmination of the period of unjustified investment brought about by the extension of credit. The projects which owe their existence to the fact that they once appeared "profitable" in the artificial conditions created on the market by the extension of credit and the increase in prices which resulted from it, have ceased to be "profitable." The capital invested in these enterprises is lost to the extent that it is locked in. The economy must adapt itself to these losses and to the situation that they bring about. In this case the thing to do, first of all, is to curtail consumption and, by economizing, to build up new capital funds in order to make the productive apparatus conform to the actual wants and not to artificial wants which could never be manifested and considered as real except as a consequence of the false calculation of "profitability" based on the extension of credit.

The artificial "boom" had been brought on by the extension of credit and by lowering of the rate of interest consequent on the intervention of the banks. During the period of credit extension, it is true that the banks progressively raised the rate of interest; from a purely arithmetical point of view it ends up higher than it had been at the beginning of the boom. This raising of the rate of interest is nevertheless insufficient to reestablish equilibrium on the market and put a stop to the unhealthy boom. For in a market where the prices are rising continually, gross interest must include in addition to interest on capital in the strict sense—i.e., the net rate of interest—still another element representing a compensation for the rise in prices arising during the period of the loan. If the prices rise in a continuous manner and if the borrower as a result gains a supplementary profit from the sale of the merchandise which he bought with the borrowed money, he will be disposed to pay a higher rate of interest than he would have paid in a period of stable prices; the capitalist, on the other hand, will not be disposed to lend under these conditions, unless the interest includes a compensation for the losses which the diminution in the purchasing power of money entails for creditors. If the banks do not take account of these conditions in setting the gross interest rate they demand, their rate ought to be considered as being maintained artificially at too low a level, even if from a purely arithmetical point of view it appears much higher than that which prevailed under "normal" conditions. Thus in Germany an interest rate of several hundred per cent could be considered too low in the autumn of 1923 because of the accelerated depreciation of the mark.

Once the reversal of the trade cycle sets in following the change in banking policy, it becomes very difficult to obtain loans because of the general restriction of credit. The rate of interest consequently rises very rapidly as a result of a sudden panic. Presently, it will fall again. It is a well-known phenomenon, indeed, that in a period of depressions a very low rate of interest—considered from the arithmetical point of view—does not succeed in stimulating economic activity. The cash reserves of individuals and of banks grow, liquid funds accumulate, yet the depression continues. In the present [1936] crisis, the accumulation of these "inactive" gold reserves has for a particular reason, taken on inordinate proportions. As is natural, capitalists wish to avoid the risk of losses from the devaluations contemplated by various governments. Given that the considerable monetary risks which the possession of bonds or of other interest-bearing securities entail are not compensated by a corresponding increase of the rate of interest, capitalists prefer to hold their funds in a form that permits them, in such a case, to protect their money from the losses inherent in an eventual devaluation by a rapid conversion to a currency not immediately menaced by the prospect of devaluation. This is the very simple reason why capitalists today are reluctant to tie themselves, through permanent investments, to a particular currency. This is why they allow their bank accounts to grow even though they return only very little interest, and hoard gold, which not only pays no interest, but also involves storage expenses.

Another factor which is helping to prolong the present period of depression is the rigidity of wages. Wages increase in periods of expansion. In periods of contraction they ought to fall, not only in money terms, but in real terms as well. By successfully preventing the lowering of wages during a period of depression, the policy of the trade unions makes unemployment a massive and persistent phenomenon. Moreover, this policy postpones the recovery indefinitely. A normal situation cannot return until prices and wages adapt themselves to the quantity of money in circulation.

Public opinion is perfectly right to see the end of the boom and the crisis as a consequence of the policy of the banks. The banks could undoubtedly have delayed the unfavorable developments for some further time. They could have continued their policy of credit expansion for a while. But—as we have already seen—they could not have persisted in it indefinitely without risking the complete collapse of the monetary system. The boom brought about by the banks' policy of extending credit must necessarily end sooner or later. Unless they are willing to let their policy completely destroy the monetary and credit system, the banks themselves must cut it short before the catastrophe occurs. The longer the period of credit expansion and the longer the banks delay in changing their policy, the worse will be the consequences of the malinvestments and of the inordinate speculation characterizing the boom; and as a result the longer will be the period of depression and the more uncertain the date of recovery and return to normal economic activity.

It has often been suggested to "stimulate" economic activity and to "prime the pump" by recourse to a new extension of credit which would allow the depression to be ended and bring about a recovery or at least a return to normal conditions; the advocates of this method forget, however, that even though it might overcome the difficulties of the moment, it will certainly produce a worse situation in a not too distant future.

Finally, it will be necessary to understand that the attempts to artificially lower the rate of interest which arises on the market, through an expansion of credit, can only produce temporary results, and that the initial recovery will be followed by a deeper decline which will manifest itself as a complete stagnation of commercial and industrial activity. The economy will not be able to develop harmoniously and smoothly unless all artificial measures that interfere with the level of prices, wages, and interest rates, as determined by the free play of economic forces, are renounced once and for all.

It is not the task of the banks to remedy the consequences of the scarcity of capital or the effects of wrong economic policy by extension of credit. It is certainly unfortunate that the return to a normal economic situation today is delayed by the pernicious policy of shackling commerce, by armaments and by the only too justified fear of war, not to mention the rigidity of wages. But it is not by banking measures and credit expansion that this situation will be corrected.

In the preceding pages I have given only a brief and necessarily insufficient sketch of the monetary theory of economic crises. It is unfortunately impossible for me in the limits set by this article to enter into greater detail; those who are interested in the subject will be able to find more in the various publications I have mentioned.

Money and the Business Cycle

Gottfried Haberler

I

If I speak of the business cycle during this lecture I do not think only or primarily of such financial and economic earthquakes as we have experienced during the last few years all over the world. It would perhaps be more interesting to talk about these dramatic events—of speculation, brokers' loans, collapse of the stock exchange, wholesale bankruptcies, panics, acute financial crises of an external or internal sort, gold drains, and the economic and political repercussions of all this. I shall, however, resist the temptation to make what I have to say dramatic and shall try instead to get down to the more fundamental economic movements which underlie those conspicuous phenomena which I have indicated.

This essay was originally published in *Gold and Monetary Stabilization* (Lectures on the Harris Foundation), Quincy Wright, ed. (Chicago: University of Chicago Press, 1932).

For a complete understanding of the business cycle it is absolutely indispensable to distinguish between a primary and fundamental and a secondary and accidental movement. The fundamental appearance of the business cycle is a wavelike movement of business activity—if I may be allowed to use for the moment this rather vague expression. The development of our modern economic life is not an even and continuous growth; it is interrupted, not only by external disturbances like wars and similar catastrophes, but shows an inherent discontinuity; periods of rapid progress are followed by periods of stagnation.

The attention of the economists was first caught by those secondary and accidental phenomena—glaring breakdowns and financial panics. They tried to explain them in terms of individual accidents, mistakes, and misguided speculations of the leaders of those banks and business firms which were primarily involved. But the regular recurrence of these accidents during the nineteenth century brought home to the economists that they had not isolated accidents before them but symptoms of a severe disease, which affects the whole economic body.

During the second half of the nineteenth century there was a marked tendency for these disturbances to become milder. Especially those conspicuous events, breakdowns, bankruptcies, and panics became less numerous, and there were even business cycles from which they were entirely absent. Before the war, it was the general belief of economists that this tendency would persist and that such dramatic breakdowns and panics as the nineteenth century had witnessed belonged definitely to the past.

Now, the present depression shows that we rejoiced too hastily, that we have not yet got rid of this scourge of the capitalistic system.

But, nevertheless, so much can be and must be learned from the experience of the past: if we want a deeper insight into the inner mechanism of our capitalistic system which makes for its cyclical movements, we must try to explain the fundamental phenomenon, abstracting from these accidental events, which might be absent or present.

If we disregard these secondary phenomena, the business cycle presents itself as a periodic up and down of general business activity, or, to put it now in a more precise form, of the volume of production. The secular growth of production does not show a continuous, uninterrupted trend upward but a wavelike movement around its average annual increase. It does not make a great difference whether the downward swings of these business waves are characterized by an absolute fall of the volume of production or just by a decrease of the rate of growth.

In this lecture I am not concerned with the ingenuous devices which statisticians have invented to isolate the cyclical movements from other periodic or erratic movements on which they are superimposed, or which are superimposed on them. I assume, first, that we have such a thing as a business cycle, which is not identical with seasonal movements within the year and erratic irregular disturbances caused by wars, periods of government inflation, and the like; it is necessary to state this, because even the existence of the phenomenon under consideration has been doubted. Secondly, I assume that we have been able to isolate this movement statistically.

Our chief concern will be with the explanation of this movement and especially with the role of money in the widest sense of the term, including credit and bank money.

II

There is hardly any explanation of the business cycle—I hesitate a little to say "theory of the business cycle," because many people have developed a certain prejudice against this term—in which the monetary factor does not play a very decisive role. The following consideration shows that this must necessarily be so: Still abstracting from the previously mentioned accessory phenomena, one of the most outstanding external symptoms of the business cycle is the rise of prices during prosperity and the fall of prices during depression. On the other hand, there is an increase of the volume of production during the upward and a decrease during the downward swing. But not only more commodities are produced and sold but also in other branches of the economy there is an increase of transactions—e.g., on the stock exchange. Therefore, we can safely say there is a considerable increase of the volume of payments during the upward swing of the cycle and a distinct decrease of this volume during depression.

Now, it is clear that, in order to handle this increased volume of payments, an augmentation of the means of payment is necessary—means of payment in the widest sense of the term. One of the following things must happen:

(a) An increase of gold and legal tender money.

(b) An increase of banknotes.

(c) An increase of bank deposits and bank credits.

(d) An increase in the circulation of checks, bills, and other means of payment which are regularly or occasionally substituted for ordinary money.

(e) An increase of the velocity of circulation of one or all of these means of payments.

I do not claim that this enumeration is exhaustive or quite systematic. It is largely a matter of terminological convenience, as one likes to express oneself. One writer prefers to call bank deposits, on which checks may be drawn, money, bank money, credit money. Other writers restrict the term "money" to legal-tender money and speak then of bank deposits as means to save money or to make it more efficient in making payments by increasing its velocity of circulation. Still others have an aversion against the term "velocity of circulation" and prefer to speak of changes in the requirement for money and means of payment.

Without going more deeply into these technical details, it is, I hope, clear that there must occur in one way or another during the upward swing of the cycle an expansion of the means of payment and during the downward swing a corresponding contraction.

No serious theory, no explanation of the cycle, can afford to overlook, disregard, or deny this fact. Differences can arise only (a) in respect to the particular way in which the expansion takes place—whether it is primarily an increase in the quantity of credit money or legal-tender money or gold or just of the velocity of circulation of one of these—and (b) as to the causal sequence.

As to the causal relation, broadly speaking, two possibilities seem to be open:

1. One might assume that the impulse comes from the side of money, that the circulation is expanded by a deliberate action of the banks or other monetary authority, and that this sets the whole chain of events going, or

2. One may hold the opinion that the monetary authorities take a passive role; that the initiative comes from the commodity side, that changes of demand for certain commodities, changes

in the structure of production, inventions and improvements, large crops, or psychological forces, a wave of optimism and pessimism—that one of these phenomena and its repercussions makes for an increase or decrease of the volume of production, and that this, in turn, draws into circulation a greater amount of means of payment. The greater flow of goods induces a larger flow of money.

The theories of the first group, which maintain that the active cause of the cycle lies on the side of money, may be called "monetary theories" of the business cycle. In a wider sense, however, we may include in the group of monetary theorists also all those who admit that the impulse might also come from the commodity side, but hold that an appropriate policy of the monetary authorities, an effective and elastic regulation of the volume of the circulating medium, can forestall every serious disturbance.

As you all know, the most frequently recommended criterion for such a policy is the "stabilization of the price level" in the one or other of the many meanings of this ambiguous term. You all will agree that it is impossible to discuss this problem exhaustively in one hour. So I shall confine myself to pointing out the insufficiencies of this type of monetary theory and of its recommendations for the remedy of the business cycle, which center around changes in the price level. I shall try, then, to indicate a more refined monetary theory of the cycle, which has been developed in the last few years, although it is not so well known in this country as it deserves to be. This refined theory seems to explain some features of the cycle, especially of the last one, which are not entirely compatible with the cruder form of the monetary approach, which identifies monetary influences with changes in the general price level.

III

The traditional monetary theory, which is represented by such well-known writers as the Swedish economist Professor Cassel and Mr. Hawtrey of the English treasury, regards the upward and the downward swing of the business cycle as a replica of a simple government inflation or deflation. To be sure, it is—as a rule—a much milder form of inflation or deflation, but at the root it is exactly the same. Mr. Hawtrey states this quite uncompromisingly in his famous dictum: "The trade cycle is a purely monetary phenomenon" and is, in principle, the same as the inflation during the war and the deflation, that is to say, the reduction of the amount of circulating medium, which was deliberately undertaken by certain governments to approach or to restore the post-war parity of their currencies.

Hawtrey recognizes and stresses, of course, the difference in degree between the two types of inflation and deflation, namely, that the expansion and contraction in the course of the business cycle is chiefly produced by maladjustment of the discount rate, which is not the way in which a government inflation is brought about. It is today an almost generally accepted doctrine, that a lowering of the discount rate by the banking system, especially by the central banks, induces people to borrow more, so that the amount of the circulating medium increases and prices rise. A raising of the discount rate has the opposite effect—it tends to depress prices or, if they were rising, to put a brake on the upward movement. I know, of course, that this bare statement needs some qualifications, I trust, however, that before so competent an audience it will suffice to say that this is literally true only if the influence of the change in the discount rate is not compensated by any other force which changes the willingness of businessmen to borrow. But, given all these other circumstances, that is to say, *ceteris paribus*, a change in the discount rate will have the indicated effect on prices. In any given situation there is one rate which keeps the price level constant. If the rate is forced below this equilibrium rate, prices have a tendency to rise; if the rate is raised above the equilibrium rate, prices tend to fall.

Now, according to Mr. Hawtrey, there is a tendency in our banking system to keep the interest rate too low during the upward swing of the cycle; then prices rise, we get a credit inflation, and sooner or later the banks are forced to take steps to protect their reserves—they increase the rate and bring about the crisis and the depression.

There is no time here to go into details, to discuss the ingenious explanation which Mr. Hawtrey offers for the fact that banks always go too far, that they swing like a pendulum from one extreme to the other and do not stop at the equilibrium rate. The reason which Mr. Hawtrey gives for this is different from the one which Professor Irving Fisher and other writers of this group have to offer. What they all have in common is that the disturbing factors act through changes of the price level. It is through changes of the price level that expansion and contraction of credit and money act upon the economic system, and they all believe that stability of the price level is the sufficient criterion of a rational regulation of credit. If it were possible to keep the price level stable, prosperity would never be followed by depression. If the price level is allowed to rise and the inevitable reaction to come, it would be possible to end the depression and to restore equilibrium, if one could stop the fall of prices.

Let me now indicate briefly why this explanation seems to me insufficient. Or, to put it in other words, I shall try to show that (a) the price level is frequently a misleading guide to monetary policy and that its stability is no sufficient safeguard against crises and depressions, because (b) a credit expansion has a much deeper and more fundamental influence on the whole economy, especially on the structure of production, than that expressed in the mere change of the price level.

The principal defect of those theories is that they do not distinguish between a fall of prices which is *due to an actual contraction* of the circulating medium and a fall of prices which is caused by *lowering of cost* as a consequence of inventions and technological improvements. (I must, however, mention that this particular criticism does not apply to Mr. Hawtrey, who, by a peculiar interpretation of the term "price level," recognizes this distinction, although he does not seem to draw the necessary conclusions.)

It is true, if there is an absolute decrease of the quantity of money, demand will fall off, prices will have to go down, and a serious depression will be the result. Normal conditions will return only after all prices have been lowered, including the prices of the factors of production, especially wages. This may be a long and painful process, because some prices, e.g., wages, are rigid and some prices and debts are definitely fixed for a long time and cannot be altered at all.

From this, however, it does not follow that the same is true if prices fall because of a lowering of costs. It is now generally accepted that the period preceding the present depression was characterized by the fact that many technological improvements, especially in the production of raw materials and agricultural products, but also in the field of manufacture, took place on a large scale.

The natural thing in such a situation would be for prices to fall gradually, and apparently such a fall of prices cannot have the same bad consequence as a fall of prices brought about by a decrease of the amount of money. We could speak, perhaps, of a "relative deflation" of the quantity of money, relative in respect to the flow of goods, in opposition to an "absolute deflation."

Especially, those writers who stress the scarcity of gold as a cause for the present depression are guilty of overlooking the radical difference between an *absolute* and a *relative* deflation. A scarcity of gold could result only in a *relative* deflation, which could never have such disastrous results as the present depression. Of a more indirect way in which the "smallness" of the annual output of gold has perhaps to do with—I do not venture to say "is the cause of"—the acuteness of the present depression and the vehemence of the price fall, I shall say more later.

Now, as I said already, during the years 1924–27 and 1928 we experienced an unprecedented growth of the volume of production. Commodity prices, on the other hand, as measured by the wholesale price index, were fairly stable, as everybody knows. From this it follows, and direct statistical investigations have verified it, that the volume of the circulating medium had been increased. We could say, there was a "relative inflation," that is, an expansion of means of payment, which did not result in an increase of commodity prices, because it was just large enough to compensate for the effect of a parallel increase of the volume of production.

There is now an obvious presumption that it was precisely this relative inflation which brought about all the trouble. If this were so—and it seems to me that it is very probable—it would be plain that the price level is a misleading guide for monetary policy and that there are monetary influences at work on the economic system that do not find an adequate expression in a change of the price level, at least as measured by the wholesale price index. And, in fact, there are such very far-reaching influences of certain monetary changes on the economic system—they may express themselves in a change of the price level or not—which have been wholly overlooked by the traditional monetary explanation, although the external symptoms of this influence have been well recognized (but differently interpreted) by certain non-monetary theories and descriptive studies of the business cycle.

IV

These changes which I have in mind and shall now try to analyze are changes of what I shall call *the vertical structure of production*, brought about by changes in the supply of credit for productive purposes. If we have to analyze an economic system, we can make a horizontal or vertical cross-section through it. A horizontal cross-section would exhibit different branches or lines of industry as differentiated by the consumption goods, which are the final result of these different branches: there, we have the food industry, including agriculture, the clothing industry, the show industry, etc. Industries which produce producer's goods—say, the iron and steel industry—belong simultaneously to different branches in this horizontal sense, because iron and steel are used in the production of many or of all consumer's goods. The old statement that a *general* overproduction is unthinkable, that we can never have too much of all goods, because human wants are insatiable, but that serious disproportionalities might develop in consequence of a partial overproduction—this statement relates principally to the horizontal structure of production. Disproportionality in this sense means that, for one reason or another, the appropriate proportion of productive resources devoted to different branches of industry has been disturbed—that, e.g., the automobile industry is overdeveloped, that more capital and labor has been invested in this industry than is justified by the comparative demand for the product of this industry and for other industrial products. I hope it is now pretty clear what I mean by horizontal structure and horizontal disproportionalities of production.

We make, on the other hand, a vertical cross-section through an economic system, if we follow every finished good, ready for consumption, up through the different phases of production and note how many stages a particular good has to pass through before it reaches the final consumer. Take, e.g., a pair of shoes and trace its economic family tree. Our path leads us from the retailer via the wholesale merchant to the shoe factory; and, taking up one of the different threads which come together at this point, say, a sewing machine used for the fabrication of shoes, we are led to the machine industry, the steel plant, and eventually to the coal and iron mine. If we follow another strand, it leads us to the farm which bred the cattle from which the leather was taken. And besides, there are many intermediate stages interpolated between these major phases of the productive process, namely, the various transportation services. Every good has to pass through many successive stages of preparation before the finishing touches are applied and it eventually reaches the final consumer. It takes a considerable length of time to follow one particular piece through this whole process, from the source of this stream to the mouth where it flows out and disappears in the bottomless sea of consumption. But, when the whole process is once completed and every one of the successive stages is properly equipped with fixed and circulating capital, we may expect a continuous flow of consumer's goods.

Now, in the equipment of these successive stages of production, the capital stock of a country, which has been accumulated during centuries, is embodied. The amount of accumulated capital is a measure of the length of the stream. In a rich country this stream is much shorter, and the volume of output correspondingly smaller. If, during a time of economic progress, capital is accumulated and invested, new stages of production are added, or, in technical economic parlance, the process of production is lengthened, it becomes more roundabout. If you compare the way in which we produce today with the methods of our fathers, or the productive process of a rich country with the one of a poor country, innumerable examples can be found.

But what has this to do with the business cycle? Now, when I spoke of the vertical structure of production and the influence of monetary forces upon it, I thought of a lengthening and shortening of the productive process. Obviously, just as there must be a certain proportion between the different horizontal branches of industry, there must also be a certain relation of the productive resources—labor and capital—which are devoted to the upper and lower stages of production respectively, to the current production of consumer's goods by means of the existing productive apparatus, and to the increase of this apparatus for the increased future production of consumer's goods.

If, e.g., too much labor is used for lengthening the process and too small an amount for current consumption, we shall get a maladjustment of the vertical structure of production. And it can be shown that certain monetary influences, concretely, a credit expansion by the banks which lowers the rate of interest below that rate which would prevail if only those sums which are deliberately saved by the public from their current income come on the capital-market—it can be shown that such an artificial decrease of the rate of interest will induce the business leaders to indulge in an excessive lengthening of the process of production, in other words, in over-investments. As the finishing of a productive process takes a considerable period of time, it turns out only too late that these newly initiated processes are too long. A reaction is inevitably produced—how, we shall see at once—which raises the rate of interest again to its natural level or even higher. Then these new investments are no longer profitable, and it becomes impossible to finish the new roundabout ways of production. They have to be abandoned, and productive resources are returned to the older, shorter methods of production. This process of adjustment of the vertical structure of production, which necessarily implies the loss of large amounts of fixed capital which is invested in those longer processes and cannot be shifted, takes place during, and constitutes the essence of, the period of depression.

Unfortunately, it is impossible to discuss here all the steps of this process and to compare them with the corresponding phases of the business cycle of which they are the picture and explanation. I hope it will be possible to give you a clear idea of what happens in our capitalistic societies during the business cycle by means of a comparison with a corresponding event in a communistic economy.

What the Russians are doing now, or trying to do—the five-year plan—is nothing else but an attempt to increase by a desperate effort the roundaboutness of production and, by means of this, to increase in the future the production of consumer's goods. Instead of producing consumer's goods, with the existing primitive methods, they have curtailed production for immediate consumption purposes to the indispensable minimum. Instead of shoes and houses they produce power plants, steel works, try to improve the transportation system, in a word, build up a productive apparatus which will turn out consumption goods only after a considerable period of time.

Now, suppose that it becomes impossible to carry through this ambitious plan. Assume the government comes to the conclusion that the population cannot stand the enormous strain, or that a revolution threatens to break out, or that by a popular vote it is decided to change the policy. In any such case, if they are forced to give up the newly initiated roundabout ways of production and to produce consumer's goods as quickly as possible, they will have to stop the building of their power plants and steel works and tractor factories and, instead of that, try to produce hurriedly simple implements and tools to increase the output of food and shoes and houses. That would mean an enormous loss of capital, sunk in those now abandoned works.

Now, what in a communistic society is done upon a decision of the supreme economic council is in our individualistic society brought about by the collective but independent action of the individuals and carried out by the price mechanism. If many people, individuals or corporations, decide to save, to restrict, for some time, their consumption, the demand for and production of consumer's goods declines, productive resources are shifted to the upper stages of production, and the process of production is being lengthened.

If we rely on voluntary saving we can assume that during every year approximately the same proportion of the national income will be saved—although not always by the same individuals. Then we have a steady flow of savings, and the adjustment of production does not take place in terms of actual shifts of invested productive resources but in terms of a lasting deflection of the flow of productive resources into other channels.

There is no reason why this should not go on smoothly and continuously. Violent fluctuations are introduced by the influence of the banks in this process. The effect of the voluntary decision of the public to save, i.e., to divert productive resources from the current production of consumption goods to the lengthening of the process, can be produced also by the banking system. If the banks create credit and place it at the disposal of certain business men who wish to use it for productive purposes, that part of the money stream, which is directed to the upper stages of production, is increased. More productive resources will be diverted from the current production of consumer's goods to the lengthening of the process than corresponds to the voluntary decision of the members of the economic community. This is what economists speak of as forced saving. First everything goes all right. But very soon prices begin to rise, because those firms who have got the new money use it to bid away factors of production—labor and working capital—from those concerns which were engaged in producing consumption goods. Wages and prices go up, and a restriction of consumption is imposed on those who are not able to increase their money income. If through previous investment of voluntary savings there is already a tendency for the price level to fall, the new credit instead of resulting in an absolute rise of prices may simply offset the price fall which would otherwise take place.

But, after some time, a reaction sets in, which tends to restore the old arrangement that has been distorted by the injection of money. The new money becomes income in the hands of the factors which have been hired away from the lower stages of production, and the receivers of this additional income will probably adhere to their habitual proportion of saving and spending, that is, they will try to increase their consumption again.

If they do this, the previous proportion of the money streams directed to the purchase of consumer's goods and of producer's goods will be restored. For some time it might be possible to overcome this countertendency and to continue the policy of expansion by making new injections of credit.

But this attempt would lead to a progressive rise of prices and must be given up sooner or later. Then the old proportion of demand for consumer's goods and producer's goods will be definitely restored. The consequence is that those firms in the lower stages of production, which had been forced to curtail their production somewhat, because factors have been hired away, will in turn be able to draw away productive resources from the higher stages. The new roundabout ways of production, which have been undertaken under the artificial stimulus of a credit expansion, or at least a part of them, become unprofitable. They will be discontinued, and the crisis and depression has its start. It could be otherwise only if the new processes were already finished when the additional money has become income and comes onto the market for consumer's goods. In this case, the additional demand would find additional supply; to the increased flow of money would correspond an increased flow of goods. This is, however, almost impossible, because, as Mr. Robertson has shown, the period of production is much longer than the period of circulation of money. The new money is bound to come on the market for consumption goods much earlier than the new proc-esses are completed and turn out goods ready for consumption.

V

This explanation of the slump, of which I have been able to indicate here only the bare outline, could, of course, be elaborated and has been elaborated. (Compare especially

Hayek, *Prices and Production* [New York: Augustus M. Kelley, 1967]). If this interpretation of the crisis and of the breakdown of a large part of the structure of production is correct, it seems then comparatively easy to explain the further events in more familiar terms. Such an initial breakdown must have very serious repercussions. In our highly complicated credit economy where every part of the system is connected with every other, directly or indirectly, by contractual bonds, every disturbance at one point spreads at once to others. If some banks—those nerve centers where innumerable strands of credit relations come together—are involved and become bankrupt, a wave of pessimism is bound to come: as a secondary phenomenon a credit deflation is likely to be the consequence of the general distrust and nervousness. All these things, upon which the traditional monetary doctrine builds its entire explanation, will make things even worse than they are, and it may very well be that this secondary wave of depression, which is induced by the more fundamental maladjustment, will grow to an overwhelming importance. This depends, however, largely upon the concrete circumstances of the case in hand, upon the peculiar features of the credit organization, on psychological factors, and need not bear a definite proportion of the magnitude of the "real" dislocation of the structure of production.

This is the place to say a few words about an indirect connection between the alleged insufficient supply of gold and the present depression. It is undoubtedly true that since before the war the quantity of gold has not increased so much as the volume of payments. To maintain a price level, roughly 50 percent higher than before the war, was possible only by building a comparatively much larger credit structure on the existing stock of gold. After the process of inflation has once been completed, this should not cause troubles—in normal times. In times of acute financial crisis, when confidence vanishes, and when runs and panics make their appearance, such a system becomes, however, extremely dangerous. If the means of payment consist principally of gold and gold-covered notes and certificates, there is no danger that suddenly a large part of the circulating medium may be annihilated. A world-system of payments, however, which relies to a large proportion on credit money, is subject to rapid deflation, if this airy credit structure is once shaken and crushed down.

For example, the adoption of a gold-exchange standard by many countries amounts to erecting a daring credit superstructure on the existing gold stock of the world; this structure may easily break down, if these countries abandon the gold-exchange standard and re-adopt an old-fashioned gold standard.

It would be, however, entirely wrong to conclude from this that we have to blame the niggardliness of nature, that the situation would necessarily be quite different, if by chance, gold production had been much larger during the last twenty years. Other factors are responsible, principally the inflation during and after the war. By means of such a monetary policy it is always possible to drive any stock of gold, however large it may be, out of the country. The natural thing is then to substitute later a gold-exchange standard for the abandoned gold standard, which means, as I have said already, the erection of a credit structure on the existing stock of gold.

Therefore, if the annual output of gold had been larger than it actually was, the difference would have been only this: the credit structure too would have become larger, and we would have started in for the last boom from a higher price level. If this is a correct guess of what would have happened—and it seems to me very probable—the economic consequences of the last period of credit expansion, 1927–29, and the present deflation would have been exactly the same.

It is of vital importance to distinguish between these additional, secondary, and accidental disturbances and the primary "real" maladjustment of the process of production. If it were only a wave of pessimism and absolute deflation which caused the trouble, it should be possible to get rid of it very quickly. After all, a deflation, however strong it may be, and by whatever circumstances it may have been made possible and aggravated, can be stopped by drastic inflationary methods within a comparatively short period of time.

If we have, however, once realized that at the bottom of these surface phenomena lies a far-reaching dislocation of productive resources, we must lose confidence in all the economic and monetary quacks who are going around these days preaching inflationary measures which would bring almost instant relief.

If we accept the proposition that the productive apparatus is out of gear, that great shifts of labor and capital are necessary to restore equilibrium, then it is emphatically not true that the business cycle is a purely monetary phenomenon, as Mr. Hawtrey would have it; this is not true, although monetary forces have brought about the whole trouble. Such a dislocation of real physical capital, as distinguished from purely monetary changes, can in no case be cured in a very short time.

I do not deny that we can and must combat the secondary phenomenon—an exaggerated pessimism and an unjustified deflation. I cannot go into this matter here, I only wish to say that we should not expect too much of a more or less symptomatic treatment, and, on the other hand, we must be careful not to produce again that artificial disproportion of the money streams, directed toward consumption and production goods, which led to overinvestment and produced the whole trouble. The worst thing we could do is a one-sided strengthening of the purchasing power of the consumer, because it was precisely this disproportional increase of demand for consumer's goods which precipitated the crisis.

It is a great advantage of this more refined monetary explanation of the business cycle, over the traditional one, to have cleared up these non-monetary, "real" changes due to monetary forces. In doing so, it has bridged the gap between the monetary and non-monetary explanation; it has taken out the elements of truth contained in each of them and combined them into one coherent system. It takes care of the well-established fact that every boom period is characterized by an extension of investments of fixed capital. It is primarily the construction of fixed capital and of the principal materials used for this—iron and steel—where the largest changes occur, the greatest expansion during the boom and the most violent contractions in the depression.

This fact, which has been stressed by all descriptive studies of the business cycle, has not been used by the traditional monetary explanations, which run in terms of changes in the price level and look at real dislocations of the structure of production, if they regard it at all, as an unimportant accidental matter. The explanation, which I have indicated, not only describes this fact as does the so-called non-monetary explanation of the cycle, but explains it. If the rate of interest is lowered, all kinds of investments come into the reach of practical consideration. May I be allowed to quote an example given by Mr. Keynes in a lecture before the Harris

Foundation Institute last year. "No one believes that it will pay to electrify the railway system of Great Britain on the basis of borrowing at 5 percent. . . . At 3 1/2 percent it is impossible to dispute that it will be worthwhile. So it must be with endless other technical projects."[1] It is clear that especially those branches of industry are favored by a reduction of the rate of interest which employ a large amount of fixed capital, as, for example, railroads, power plants, etc. In their cost-account, interest charges play an important role. But there is an indisputable general tendency to replace labor by machinery, if capital becomes cheap. That is to say, more labor and working capital is used to produce machines, railroads, power plants—comparatively less for current production of con-sumption goods. In technical economic parlance: the round-aboutness of production is increased. The crucial point and also the point of deviation from Mr. Keynes's analysis is to understand well that a reaction must inevitably set in, if this productive expansion is not financed by real, voluntary saving of individuals or corporations but by *ad hoc* created credit. And it is practically very important—the last boom should have brought this home to us—that a stable commodity price level is not a sufficient safeguard against such an artificial stimulation of an expansion of production. In other words, that a relative credit inflation, in the above-defined meaning

---

[1] *Unemployment as a World Problem* (Chicago, 1931), p. 39.

of the term, will induce the same counter-movements as an absolute inflation.

I hope that I have been able to give you a tolerably clear idea of this improved monetary explanation of the business cycle. Once more I must ask you not to take as a complete exposition what can be only a brief indication. A sufficiently detailed discussion of the case could be only undertaken in a big volume. Therefore, I beg you to suspend your final judgment until the case has been more fully presented to you. Only one objection I should like to anticipate. It is true this theory suffers from a serious disadvantage: it is so much more complicated than the traditional monetary explanation. But I venture to say that this is not the fault of this theory, but due to the malice of the object. Unfortunately, facts are not always so simple as many people would like to have them.

Economic Depressions:
Their Cause and Cure

Murray N. Rothbard

We live in a world of euphemism. Undertakers have become "morticians," press agents are now "public relations counsellors" and janitors have all been transformed into "superintendents." In every walk of life, plain facts have been wrapped in cloudy camouflage.

No less has this been true of economics. In the old days, we used to suffer nearly periodic economic crises, the sudden onset of which was called a "panic," and the lingering trough period after the panic was called "depression."

The most famous depression in modern times, of course, was the one that began in a typical financial panic in 1929 and lasted until the advent of World War II. After the disaster of 1929, economists and politicians resolved that this must never happen again. The easiest way of succeeding at this resolve was, simply to define "depressions" out of existence. From

This essay was originally published as a minibook by the Constitutional Alliance of Lansing, Michigan, 1969.

that point on, America was to suffer no further depressions. For when the next sharp depression came along, in 1937–38, the economists simply refused to use the dread name, and came up with a new, much softer-sounding word: "recession." From that point on, we have been through quite a few recessions, but not a single depression.

But pretty soon the word "recession" also became too harsh for the delicate sensibilities of the American public. It now seems that we had our last recession in 1957–58. For since then, we have only had "downturns," or, even better, "slowdowns," or "sidewise movements." So be of good cheer; from now on, depressions and even recessions have been outlawed by the semantic fiat of economists; from now on, the worst that can possibly happen to us are "slowdowns." Such are the wonders of the "New Economics."

For 30 years, our nation's economists have adopted the view of the business cycle held by the late British economist, John Maynard Keynes, who created the Keynesian, or the "New," Economics in his book, *The General Theory of Employment, Interest, and Money*, published in 1936. Beneath their diagrams, mathematics, and inchoate jargon, the attitude of Keynesians toward booms and bust is simplicity, even naivete, itself. If there is inflation, then the cause is supposed to be "excessive spending" on the part of the public; the alleged cure is for the government, the self-appointed stabilizer and regulator of the nation's economy, to step in and force people to spend less, "sopping up their excess purchasing power" through increased taxation. If there is a recession, on the other hand, this has been caused by insufficient private spending, and the cure now is for the government to increase its own spending, preferably through deficits, thereby adding to the nation's aggregate spending stream.

The idea that increased government spending or easy money is "good for business" and that budget cuts or harder money is "bad" permeates even the most conservative newspapers and magazines. These journals will also take for granted that it is the sacred task of the federal government to steer the economic system on the narrow road between the abysses of depression on the one hand and inflation on the other, for the free-market economy is supposed to be ever liable to succumb to one of these evils.

All current schools of economists have the same attitude. Note, for example, the viewpoint of Dr. Paul W. McCracken, the incoming chairman of President Nixon's Council of Economic Advisers. In an interview with the *New York Times* shortly after taking office [January 24, 1969], Dr. McCracken asserted that one of the major economic problems facing the new Administration is "how you cool down this inflationary economy without at the same time tripping off unacceptably high levels of unemployment. In other words, if the only thing we want to do is cool off the inflation, it could be done. But our social tolerances on unemployment are narrow." And again: "I think we have to feel our way along here. We don't really have much experience in trying to cool an economy in orderly fashion. We slammed on the brakes in 1957, but, of course, we got substantial slack in the economy."

Note the fundamental attitude of Dr. McCracken toward the economy—remarkable only in that it is shared by almost all economists of the present day. The economy is treated as a potentially workable, but always troublesome and recalcitrant patient, with a continual tendency to hive off into greater inflation or unemployment. The function of the government is to be the wise old manager and physician, ever watchful, ever tinkering to keep the economic patient in good working order. In any case, here the economic patient is clearly supposed to be the subject, and the government as "physician" the master.

It was not so long ago that this kind of attitude and policy was called "socialism"; but we live in a world of euphemism, and now we call it by far less harsh labels, such as "moderation" or "enlightened free enterprise." We live and learn.

What, then, are the causes of periodic depressions? Must we always remain agnostic about the causes of booms and busts? Is it really true that business cycles are rooted deep within the free-market economy, and that therefore some form of government planning is needed if we wish to keep the economy within some kind of stable bounds? Do booms and then busts just simply happen, or does one phase of the cycle flow logically from the other?

The currently fashionable attitude toward the business cycle stems, actually, from Karl Marx. Marx saw that, before the Industrial Revolution in approximately the late eighteenth century, there were no regularly recurring booms and depressions. There would be a sudden economic crisis whenever some king made war or confiscated the property of his subject; but there was no sign of the peculiarly modern phenomena of general and fairly regular swings in business fortunes, of expansions and contractions. Since these cycles also appeared on the scene at about the same time as modern industry, Marx concluded that business cycles were an inherent feature of the capitalist market economy. All the various current schools of economic thought, regardless of their other differences and the different causes that they attribute to the cycle, agree on this vital point: That these business cycles originate somewhere deep within the free-market economy. The market economy is to blame. Karl Marx believed that the periodic depressions would get worse and worse, until the masses would be moved to revolt and destroy the system, while the modern economists believe that the government can successfully stabilize depressions and the cycle. But all parties agree that the fault lies deep within the market economy and that if anything can save the day, it must be some form of massive government intervention.

There are, however, some critical problems in the assumption that the market economy is the culprit. For "general economic theory" teaches us that supply and demand always tend to be in equilibrium in the market and that therefore prices of products as well as of the factors that contribute to production are always tending toward some equilibrium point. Even though changes of data, which are always taking place, prevent equilibrium from ever being reached, there is nothing in the general theory of the market system that would account for regular and recurring boom-and-bust phases of the business cycle. Modern economists "solve" this problem by simply keeping their general price and market theory and their business cycle theory in separate, tightly-sealed compartments, with never the twain meeting, much less integrated with each other. Economists, unfortunately, have forgotten that there is only one economy and therefore only one integrated economic theory. Neither economic life nor the structure of theory can or should be in watertight compartments; our knowledge of the economy is either one integrated whole or it is nothing. Yet most economists are content to apply totally separate and, indeed, mutually exclusive, theories for general price analysis and for business cycles. They cannot be genuine economic scientists so long as they are content to keep operating in this primitive way.

But there are still graver problems with the currently fashionable approach. Economists also do not see one particularly critical problem because they do not bother to square their business cycle and general price theories: the peculiar breakdown of the entrepreneurial function at times of economic crisis and depression. In the market economy, one of the most vital functions of the businessman is to be an "entrepreneur," a man who invests in productive methods, who buys equipment and hires labor to produce something which he is not sure will reap him any return. In short, the entrepreneurial function is the function of forecasting the uncertain future. Before embarking on any investment or line of production, the entrepreneur, or "enterpriser," must estimate present and future costs and future revenues and therefore estimate whether and how much profits he will earn from the investment. If he forecasts well and significantly better than his business competitors, he will reap profits from his investment. The better his forecasting, the higher the profits he will earn. If, on the other hand, he is a poor forecaster and overestimates the demand for his product, he will suffer losses and pretty soon be forced out of the business.

The market economy, then, is a profit-and-loss economy, in which the acumen and ability of business entrepreneurs is gauged by the profits and losses they reap. The market economy, moreover, contains a built-in mechanism, a kind of natural selection, that ensures the survival and the flourishing of the superior forecaster and the weeding-out of the inferior ones. For the more profits reaped by the better forecasters, the greater become their business responsibilities, and the more they will have available to invest in the productive system. On the other hand, a few years of making losses will drive the poorer forecasters and entrepreneurs out of business altogether and push them into the ranks of salaried employees.

If, then, the market economy has a built-in natural selection mechanism for good entrepreneurs, this means that, generally, we would expect not many business firms to be making losses. And, in fact, if we look around at the economy on an average day or year, we will find that losses are not very widespread. But, in that case, the odd fact that needs explaining is this: How is it that, periodically, in times of the onset of recessions and especially in steep depressions, the business world suddenly experiences a massive cluster of severe losses? A moment arrives when business firms, previously highly astute entrepreneurs in their ability to make profits and avoid losses, suddenly and dismayingly find themselves, almost all of them, suffering severe and unaccountable losses? How come? Here is a momentous fact that any theory of depressions must explain. An explanation such as "underconsumption"—a drop in total consumer spending—is not sufficient, for one thing, because what needs to be explained is why businessmen, able to forecast all manner of previous economic changes and developments, proved themselves totally and catastrophically unable to forecast this alleged drop in consumer demand. Why this sudden failure in forecasting ability?

An adequate theory of depressions, then, must account for the tendency of the economy to move through successive booms and busts, showing no sign of settling into any sort of smoothly moving, or quietly progressive, approximation of an equilibrium situation. In particular, a theory of depression must account for the mammoth cluster of errors which appears swiftly and suddenly at a moment of economic crisis, and lingers through the depression period until recovery. And there is a third universal fact that a theory of the cycle must account for. Invariably, the booms and busts are much more intense and severe in the "capital goods industries"—the industries making machines and equipment, the ones producing industrial raw materials or constructing industrial plants—than in the industries making consumers' goods. Here is another fact of business cycle life that must be explained—and obviously can't be explained by such theories of depression as the popular underconsumption doctrine: That consumers aren't spending enough on consumer goods. For if insufficient spending is the culprit, then how is it that retail sales are the last and the least to fall in any depression, and that depression *really* hits such industries as machine tools, capital equipment, construction, and raw materials? Conversely, it is these industries that really take off in the inflationary boom phases of the business cycle, and not those businesses serving the consumer. An adequate theory of the business cycle, then, must also explain the far greater intensity of booms and busts in the non-consumer goods, or "producers' goods," industries.

Fortunately, a correct theory of depression and of the business cycle *does* exist, even though it is universally neglected in present-day economics. It, too, has a long tradition in economic thought. This theory began with the eighteenth century Scottish philosopher and economist David Hume, and with the eminent early nineteenth century English classical economist David Ricardo. Essentially, these theorists saw that another crucial institution had developed in the mid-eighteenth century, alongside the industrial system. This was the institution of banking, with its capacity to expand credit and the money supply (first, in the form of paper money, or bank notes, and later in the form of demand deposits, or checking accounts, that are instantly redeemable in cash at the banks). It was the operations of these commercial banks which, these economists saw, held the key to the mysterious recurrent cycles of expansion and contraction, of boom and bust, that had puzzled observers since the mid-eighteenth century.

The Ricardian analysis of the business cycle went something as follows: The natural moneys emerging as such on the world free market are useful commodities, generally gold and silver. If money were confined simply to these commodities, then the economy would work in the aggregate as it does in particular markets: A smooth adjustment of supply and demand, and therefore no cycles of boom and bust. But the injection of bank credit adds another crucial and disruptive element. For the banks expand credit and therefore bank money in the form of notes or deposits which are theoretically redeemable on demand in gold, but in practice clearly are not. For example, if a bank has 1000 ounces of gold in its vaults, and it issues instantly redeemable warehouse receipts for 2500 ounces of gold, then it clearly has issued 1500 ounces more than it can possibly redeem. But so long as there is no concerted "run" on the bank to cash in these receipts, its warehouse-receipts function on the market as equivalent to gold, and therefore the bank has been able to expand the money supply of the country by 1500 gold ounces.

The banks, then, happily begin to expand credit, for the more they expand credit the greater will be their profits. This results in the expansion of the money supply within a country, say England. As the supply of paper and bank money in England increases, the money incomes and expenditures of Englishmen rise, and the increased money bids up prices of English goods. The result is inflation and a boom within the country. But this inflationary boom, while it proceeds on its merry way, sows the seeds of its own demise. For as English money supply and incomes increase, Englishmen proceed to purchase more goods from abroad. Furthermore, as English prices go up, English goods begin to lose their competitiveness with the products of other countries which have not inflated, or have been inflating to a lesser degree. Englishmen begin to buy less at home and more abroad, while foreigners buy less in England and more at home; the result is a deficit in the English balance of payments, with English exports falling sharply behind imports. But if imports exceed exports, this means that money must flow out of England to foreign countries. And what money will this be? Surely not English bank notes or deposits, for Frenchmen or Germans or Italians have little or no interest in keeping their funds locked up in English banks. These foreigners will therefore take their bank notes and deposits and present them to the English banks for redemption in gold—and gold will be the type of money that will tend to flow persistently out of the country as the English inflation proceeds on its way. But this means that English bank credit money will be, more and more, pyramiding on top of a dwindling gold base in the English bank vaults. As the boom proceeds, our hypothetical bank will expand its warehouse receipts issued from, say 2500 ounces to 4000 ounces, while its gold base dwindles to, say, 800. As this process intensifies, the banks will eventually become frightened. For the banks, after all, are obligated to redeem their liabilities in cash, and their cash is flowing out rapidly as their liabilities pile up. Hence, the banks will eventually lose their nerve, stop their credit expansion, and in order to save themselves, contract their bank loans outstanding. Often, this retreat is precipitated by bankrupting runs on the banks touched off by the public, who had also been getting increasingly nervous about the ever more shaky condition of the nation's banks.

The bank contraction reverses the economic picture; contraction and bust follow boom. The banks pull in their horns, and businesses suffer as the pressure mounts for debt repayment and contraction. The fall in the supply of bank money, in turn, leads to a general fall in English prices. As money supply and incomes fall, and English prices collapse, English goods become relatively more attractive in terms of foreign products, and the balance of payments reverses itself, with exports exceeding imports. As gold flows into the country, and as bank money contracts on top of an expanding gold base, the condition of the banks becomes much sounder.

This, then, is the meaning of the depression phase of the business cycle. Note that it is a phase that comes out of, and inevitably comes out of, the preceding expansionary boom. It is the preceding inflation that makes the depression phase necessary. We can see, for example, that the depression is the process by which the market economy adjusts, throws off the excesses and distortions of the previous inflationary boom, and reestablishes a sound economic condition. The depression is the unpleasant but necessary reaction to the distortions and excesses of the previous boom.

Why, then, does the next cycle begin? Why do business cycles tend to be recurrent and continuous? Because when the banks have pretty well recovered, and are in a sounder condition, they are then in a confident position to proceed to their natural path of bank credit expansion, and the next boom proceeds on its way, sowing the seeds for the next inevitable bust.

But if banking is the cause of the business cycle, aren't the banks also a part of the private market economy, and can't we therefore say that the free market is *still* the culprit, if only in the banking segment of that free market? The answer is No, for the banks, for one thing, would never be able to expand credit in concert were it not for the intervention and encouragement of government. For if banks were truly competitive, any expansion of credit by one bank would quickly pile up the debts of that bank in its competitors, and its competitors would quickly call upon the expanding bank for redemption in cash. In short, a bank's rivals will call upon it for redemption in gold or cash in the same way as do foreigners, except that the process is much faster and would nip any incipient inflation in the bud before it got started. Banks can only expand comfortably in unison when a Central Bank exists, essentially a governmental bank, enjoying a monopoly of government business, and a privileged position imposed by government over the entire banking system. It is only when central banking got established that the banks were able to expand for any length of time and the familiar business cycle got underway in the modern world.

The central bank acquires its control over the banking system by such governmental measures as: Making its own liabilities legal tender for all debts and receivable in taxes; granting the central bank monopoly of the issue of bank *notes*, as contrasted to deposits (in England the Bank of England, the governmentally established central bank, had a legal monopoly of bank notes in the London area); or through the outright forcing of banks to use the central bank as their client for keeping their reserves of cash (as in the United States and its Federal Reserve System). Not that the banks complain about this intervention; for it is the establishment of central banking that makes long-term bank credit expansion possible, since the expansion of Central Bank notes provides added cash reserves for the entire banking system and permits all the commercial banks to expand their credit together. Central banking works like a cozy compulsory bank cartel to expand the banks' liabilities; and the banks are now able to expand on a larger base of cash in the form of central bank notes as well as gold.

So now we see, at last, that the business cycle is brought about, not by any mysterious failings of the free market economy, but quite the opposite: By systematic intervention by government in the market process. Government intervention brings about bank expansion and inflation, and, when the inflation comes to an end, the subsequent depression-adjustment comes into play.

The Ricardian theory of the business cycle grasped the essentials of a correct cycle theory: The recurrent nature of the phases of the cycle, depression as adjustment intervention in the market rather than from the free-market economy. But two problems were as yet unexplained: Why the sudden cluster of business error, the sudden failure of the entrepreneurial function, and why the vastly greater fluctuations in the producers' goods than in the consumers' goods industries? The Ricardian theory only explained movements in the price level, in general business; there was no hint of explanation of the vastly different reactions in the capital and consumers' goods industries.

The correct and fully developed theory of the business cycle was finally discovered and set forth by the Austrian economist Ludwig von Mises, when he was a professor at the University of Vienna. Mises developed hints of his solution to the vital problem of the business cycle in his monumental *Theory of Money and Credit*, published in 1912, and still, nearly 60 years later, the best book on the theory of money and banking. Mises developed his cycle theory during the 1920s, and it was brought to the English-speaking world by Mises's leading follower, Friedrich A. von Hayek, who came from Vienna to teach at the London School of Economics in the early 1930s, and who published, in German and in English, two books which applied and elaborated the Mises cycle theory: *Monetary Theory and the Trade Cycle*, and *Prices and Production*. Since Mises and Hayek were Austrians, and also since they were in the tradition of the great nineteenth-century Austrian economists, this theory has become known in the literature as the "Austrian" (or the "monetary over-investment") theory of the business cycle.

Building on the Ricardians, on general "Austrian" theory, and on his own creative genius, Mises developed the following theory of the business cycle:

Without bank credit expansion, supply and demand tend to be equilibrated through the free price system, and no cumulative booms or busts can then develop. But then government through its central bank stimulates bank credit expansion by expanding central bank liabilities and therefore the cash reserves of all the nation's commercial banks. The banks then proceed to expand credit and hence the nation's money supply in the form of check deposits. As the Ricardians saw, this expansion of bank money drives up the prices of goods and hence causes inflation. But, Mises showed, it does something else, and something even more sinister. Bank credit expansion, by pouring new loan funds into the business world, artificially lowers the rate of interest in the economy below its free market level.

On the free and unhampered market, the interest rate is determined purely by the "time-preferences" of all the individuals that make up the market economy. For the essence of a loan is that a "present good" (money which can be used at present) is being exchanged for a "future good" (an IOU which can only be used at some point in the future). Since people always prefer money right now to the present prospect of getting the same amount of money some time in the future, the present good always commands a premium in the market over the future. This premium is the interest rate, and its height will vary according to the degree to which people prefer the present to the future, i.e., the degree of their time-preferences.

People's time-preferences also determine the extent to which people will save and invest, as compared to how much they will consume. If people's time-preferences should fall, i.e., if their degree of preference for present over future falls, then people will tend to consume less now and save and invest more; at the same time, and for the same reason, the rate of interest, the rate of time-discount, will also fall. Economic growth comes about largely as the result of falling rates of time-preference, which lead to an increase in the proportion of saving and investment to consumption, and also to a falling rate of interest.

But what happens when the rate of interest falls, not because of lower time-preferences and higher savings, but from government interference that promotes the expansion of bank credit? In other words, if the rate of interest falls artificially, due to intervention, rather than naturally, as a result of changes in the valuations and preferences of the consuming public?

What happens is trouble. For businessmen, seeing the rate of interest fall, react as they always would and must to such a change of market signals: They invest more in capital and producers' goods. Investments, particularly in lengthy and time-consuming projects, which previously looked unprofitable now seem profitable, because of the fall of the interest charge. In short, businessmen react as they would react if savings had *genuinely* increased: They expand their investment in durable equipment, in capital goods, in industrial raw material, in construction as compared to their direct production of consumer goods.

Businesses, in short, happily borrow the newly expanded bank money that is coming to them at cheaper rates; they use the money to invest in capital goods, and eventually this money gets paid out in higher rents to land, and higher wages to workers in the capital goods industries. The increased business demand bids up labor costs, but businesses think they can pay these higher costs because they have been fooled by the government-and-bank intervention in the loan market and its decisively important tampering with the interest-rate signal of the marketplace.

The problem comes as soon as the workers and land-lords—largely the former, since most gross business income is paid out in wages—begin to spend the new bank money that they have received in the form of higher wages. For the time-preferences of the public have not *really* gotten lower; the public doesn't *want* to save more than it has. So the workers set about to consume most of their new income, in short to reestablish the old consumer/saving proportions. This means that they redirect the spending back to the consumer goods industries, and they don't save and invest enough to buy the newly-produced machines, capital equipment, industrial raw materials, etc. This all reveals itself as a sudden sharp and continuing depression in the *producers' goods* industries. Once the consumers reestablished their desired consumption/investment proportions, it is thus revealed that business had invested too much in capital goods and had underinvested in consumer goods. Business had been seduced by the governmental tampering and artificial lowering of the rate of interest, and acted as if more savings were available to invest than were really there. As soon as the new bank money filtered through the system and the consumers reestablished their old proportions, it became clear that there were not enough savings to buy all the producers' goods, and that business had misinvested the limited savings available. Business had overinvested in capital goods and underinvested in consumer products.

The inflationary boom thus leads to distortions of the pricing and production system. Prices of labor and raw materials in the capital goods industries had been bid up during the boom too high to be profitable once the consumers reassert their old consumption/investment preferences. The "depression" is then seen as the necessary and healthy phase by which the market economy sloughs off and liquidates the unsound, uneconomic investments of the boom, and reestablishes those proportions between consumption and investment that are truly desired by the consumers. The depression is the painful but necessary process by which the free market sloughs off the excesses and errors of the boom and reestablishes the market economy in its function of efficient service to the mass of consumers. Since prices of factors of production have been bid too high in the boom, this means that prices of labor and goods in these capital goods industries must be allowed to fall until proper market relations are resumed.

Since the workers receive the increased money in the form of higher wages fairly rapidly, how is it that booms can go on for years without having their unsound investments revealed, their errors due to tampering with market signals become evident, and the depression-adjustment process begins its work? The answer is that booms would be very short lived if the bank credit expansion and subsequent pushing of the rate of interest below the free market level were a one-shot affair. But the point is that the credit expansion is *not* one-shot; it proceeds on and on, never giving consumers the chance to reestablish their preferred proportions of consumption and saving, never allowing the rise in costs in the capital goods industries to catch up to the inflationary rise in prices. Like the repeated doping of a horse, the boom is kept on its way and ahead of its inevitable comeuppance, by repeated doses of the stimulant of bank credit. It is only when bank credit expansion must finally stop, either because the banks are getting into a shaky condition or because the public begins to balk at the continuing inflation, that retribution finally catches up with the boom. As soon as credit expansion stops, then the piper must be paid, and the inevitable readjustments liquidate the unsound over-investments of the boom, with the reassertion of a greater proportionate emphasis on consumers' goods production.

Thus, the Misesian theory of the business cycle accounts for all of our puzzles: The repeated and recurrent nature of the cycle, the massive cluster of entrepreneurial error, the far greater intensity of the boom and bust in the producers' goods industries.

Mises, then, pinpoints the blame for the cycle on inflationary bank credit expansion propelled by the intervention of government and its central bank. What does Mises say should be done, say by government, once the depression arrives? What is the governmental role in the cure of depression? In the first place, government must cease inflating as soon as possible. It is true that this will, inevitably, bring the inflationary boom abruptly to an end, and commence the inevitable recession or depression. But the longer the government waits for this, the worse the necessary readjustments will have to be. The sooner the depression-readjustment is gotten over with, the better. This means, also, that the government must never try to prop up unsound business situations; it must never bail out or lend money to business firms in trouble. Doing this will simply prolong the agony and convert a sharp and quick depression phase into a lingering and chronic disease. The government must never try to prop up wage rates or prices of producers' goods; doing so will prolong and delay indefinitely the completion of the depression-adjustment process; it will cause indefinite and prolonged depression and mass unemployment in the vital capital goods industries. The government must not try to inflate again, in order to get out of the depression. For even if this reinflation succeeds, it will only sow greater trouble later on. The government must do nothing to encourage consumption, and it must not increase its own expenditures, for this will further increase the social consumption/investment ratio. In fact, cutting the government budget will improve the ratio. What the economy needs is not more consumption spending but more saving, in order to validate some of the excessive investments of the boom.

Thus, what the government should do, according to the Misesian analysis of the depression, is absolutely nothing. It should, from the point of view of economic health and ending the depression as quickly as possible, maintain a strict hands off, "*laissez-faire*" policy. Anything it does will delay and obstruct the adjustment process of the market; the less it does, the more rapidly will the market adjustment process do its work, and sound economic recovery ensue.

The Misesian prescription is thus the exact opposite of the Keynesian: It is for the government to keep absolute hands off the economy and to confine itself to stopping its own inflation and to cutting its own budget.

It has today been completely forgotten, even among economists, that the Misesian explanation and analysis of the depression gained great headway precisely during the Great Depression of the 1930s—the very depression that is always held up to advocates of the free market economy as the greatest single and catastrophic failure of *laissez-faire* capitalism. It was no such thing. 1929 was made inevitable by the vast bank credit expansion throughout the Western world during the 1920s: A policy deliberately adopted by the Western governments, and most importantly by the Federal Reserve System in the United States. It was made possible by the failure of the Western world to return to a genuine gold standard after World War I, and thus allowing more room for inflationary policies by government. Everyone now thinks of President Coolidge as a believer in *laissez-faire* and an unhampered market economy; he was not, and tragically, nowhere less so than in the field of money and credit. Unfortunately, the sins and errors of the Coolidge intervention were laid to the door of a non-existent free market economy.

If Coolidge made 1929 inevitable, it was President Hoover who prolonged and deepened the depression, transforming it from a typically sharp but swiftly-disappearing depression into a lingering and near-fatal malady, a malady "cured" only by the holocaust of World War II. Hoover, not Franklin Roosevelt, was the founder of the policy of the "New Deal": essentially the massive use of the State to do exactly what Misesian theory would most warn against—to prop up wage rates above their free-market levels, prop up prices, inflate credit, and lend money to shaky business positions. Roosevelt only advanced, to a greater degree, what Hoover had pioneered. The result for the first time in American history, was a nearly perpetual depression and nearly permanent mass unemployment. The Coolidge crisis had become the unprecedentedly prolonged Hoover–Roosevelt depression.

Ludwig von Mises had predicted the depression during the heyday of the great boom of the 1920s—a time, just like today, when economists and politicians, armed with a "new economics" of perpetual inflation, and with new "tools" provided by the Federal Reserve System, proclaimed a perpetual "New Era" of permanent prosperity guaranteed by our wise economic doctors in Washington. Ludwig von Mises, alone armed with a correct theory of the business cycle, was one of the very few economists to predict the Great Depression, and hence the economic world was forced to listen to him with respect. F. A. Hayek spread the word in England, and the younger English economists were all, in the early 1930s, beginning to adopt the Misesian cycle theory for their analysis of the depression—and also to adopt, of course, the strictly free-market policy prescription that flowed with this theory. Unfortunately, economists have now adopted the historical notion of Lord Keynes: That no "classical economists" had a theory of the business cycle until Keynes came along in 1936. There *was* a theory of the depression; it was the classical economic tradition; its prescription was strict hard money and *laissez-faire*; and it was rapidly being adopted, in England and even in the United States, as the accepted theory of the business cycle. (A particular irony is that the major "Austrian" proponent in the United States in the early and mid-1930s was none other than Professor Alvin Hansen, very soon to make his mark as the outstanding Keynesian disciple in this country.)

What swamped the growing acceptance of Misesian cycle theory was simply the "Keynesian Revolution"—the amazing sweep that Keynesian theory made of the economic world shortly after the publication of the *General Theory* in 1936. It is not that Misesian theory was refuted successfully; it was just *forgotten* in the rush to climb on the suddenly fashionable Keynesian bandwagon. Some of the leading adherents of the

Mises theory—who clearly knew better—succumbed to the newly established winds of doctrine, and won leading American university posts as a consequence.

But now the once arch-Keynesian London *Economist* has recently proclaimed that "Keynes is Dead." After over a decade of facing trenchant theoretical critiques and refutation by stubborn economic facts, the Keynesians are now in general and massive retreat. Once again, the money supply and bank credit are being grudgingly acknowledged to play a leading role in the cycle. The time is ripe—for a rediscovery, a renaissance, of the Mises theory of the business cycle. It can come none too soon; if it ever does, the whole concept of a Council of Economic Advisors would be swept away, and we would see a massive retreat of government from the economic sphere. But for all this to happen, the world of economics, and the public at large, must be made aware of the existence of an explanation of the business cycle that has lain neglected on the shelf for all too many tragic years.

Can We Still Avoid Inflation?

Friedrich A. Hayek

In one sense the question asked in the title of this lecture is purely rhetorical. I hope none of you has suspected me of doubting even for a moment that technically there is no problem in stopping inflation. If the monetary authorities really want to and are prepared to accept the consequences, they can always do so practically overnight. They fully control the base of the pyramid of credit, and a credible announcement that they will not increase the quantity of bank notes in circulation and bank deposits, and, if necessary, even decrease them, will do the trick. About this there is no doubt among economists. What I am concerned about is not the technical but the political possibilities. Here, indeed, we face a task so difficult that more and more people, including highly competent people, have resigned themselves to the inevitability of indefinitely continued inflation. I know in fact of no serious attempt to show how we can overcome these obstacles

This essay was originally given as a lecture before the Trustees and guests of the Foundation for Economic Education at Tarrytown, New York on May 18, 1970, and was first published in the first edition of this book.

which lie not in the monetary but in the political field. And I cannot myself claim to have a patent medicine which I am sure is applicable and effective in the prevailing conditions. But I do not regard it as a task beyond the scope of human ingenuity once the urgency of the problem is generally understood. My main aim tonight is to bring out clearly why we must stop inflation if we are to preserve a viable society of free men. Once this urgent necessity is fully understood, I hope people will also gather the courage to grasp the hot irons which must be tackled if the political obstacles are to be removed and we are to have a chance of restoring a functioning market economy.

In the elementary textbook accounts, and probably also in the public mind generally, only one harmful effect of inflation is seriously considered, that on the relations between debtors and creditors. Of course, an unforeseen depreciation of the value of money harms creditors and benefits debtors. This is important but by no means the most important effect of inflation. And since it is the creditors who are harmed and the debtors who benefit, most people do not particularly mind, at least until they realize that in modern society the most important and numerous class of creditors are the wage and salary earners and the small savers, and the representative groups of debtors who profit in the first instance are the enterprises and credit institutions.

But I do not want to dwell too long on this most familiar effect of inflation which is also the one which most readily corrects itself. Twenty years ago I still had some difficulty to make my students believe that if an annual rate of price increase of five per cent were generally expected, we would have rates of interest of 9-10 per cent or more. There still seem to be a few people who have not yet understood that rates of this sort are bound to last so long as inflation continues. Yet, so long as this is the case, and the creditors understand that only part of their gross return is net return, at least short term lenders have comparatively little ground for complaint—even though long term creditors, such as the owners of government loans and other debentures, are partly expropriated.

There is, however, another more devious aspect of this process which I must at least briefly mention at this point. It is that it upsets the reliability of all accounting practices and is bound to show spurious profits much in excess to true gains. Of course, a wise manager could allow for this also, at least in a general way, and treat as profits only what remains after he has taken into account the depreciation of money as affecting the replacement costs of his capital. But the tax inspector will not permit him to do so and insist on taxing all the pseudo-profits. Such taxation is simply confiscation of some of the substance of capital, and in the case of a rapid inflation may become a very serious matter.

But all this is familiar ground—matters of which I merely wanted to remind you before turning to the less conspicuous but, for that very reason, more dangerous effects of inflation.

The whole conventional analysis reproduced in most text-books proceeds as if a rise in average prices meant that all prices rise at the same time by more or less the same percentage, or that this at least was true of all prices determined currently on the market, leaving out only a few prices fixed by decree or long term contracts, such as public utility rates, rents and various conventional fees. But this is not true or even possible. The crucial point is that so long as the flow of money expenditure continues to grow and prices of commodities and services are driven up, the different prices must rise, not at the same time but *in succession*, and that in consequence, so long as this process continues, the prices which rise first must all the time move ahead of the others. This distortion of the whole price structure will disappear only sometime after the process of inflation has stopped. This is a fundamental point which the master of all of us, Ludwig von Mises, has never tired from emphasizing for the past sixty years. It seems nevertheless necessary to dwell upon it at some length since, as I recently discovered with some shock, it is not appreciated and even explicitly denied by one of the most distinguished living economists.[1]

That the order in which a continued increase in the money stream raises the different prices is crucial for an

---

[1] [See Professor Hayek's criticism of Sir John Hicks in his article, "Three Elucidations of the Ricardo Effect," *Journal of Political Economy* (March–April 1969): 274—ed.]

understanding of the effects of inflation was clearly seen more than two hundred years ago by David Hume—and indeed before him by Richard Cantillon. It was in order deliberately to eliminate this effect that Hume assumed as a first approximation that one morning every citizen of a country woke up to find the stock of money in his possession miraculously doubled. Even this would not really lead to an immediate rise of all prices by the same percentage. But it is not what ever really happens. The influx of the additional money into the system always takes place at some particular point. There will always be some people who have more money to spend before the others. Who these people are will depend on the particular manner in which the increase in the money stream is being brought about. It may be spent in the first instance by government on public works or increased salaries, or it may be first spent by investors mobilizing cash balances or borrowing for the purpose; it may be spent in the first instance on securities, on investment goods, on wages or on consumer's goods. It will then in turn be spent on something else by the first recipients of the additional expenditure, and so on. The process will take very different forms according to the initial source or sources of the additional money stream; and all its ramifications will soon be so complex that nobody can trace them. But one thing all these different forms of the process will have in common: that the different prices will rise, not at the same time but in succession, and that so long as the process continues some prices will always be ahead of the others and the whole structure of relative prices therefore very different from what the pure theorist describes as an equilibrium position. There will always exist what might be described as a prices gradient in favor of those commodities and services which each increment of the money stream hits first and to the disadvantage of the successive groups which it reaches only later—with the effect that what will rise as a whole will not be a level but a sort of inclined plane—if we take as normal the system of prices which existed before inflation started and which will approximately restore itself sometime after it has stopped.

To such a change in relative prices, if it has persisted for some time and comes to be expected to continue, will of course correspond a similar change in the allocation of resources: relatively more will be produced of the goods and services whose prices are now comparatively higher and relatively less of those whose prices are comparatively lower. This redistribution of the productive resources will evidently persist so long, but only so long, as inflation continues at a given rate. We shall see that this inducement to activities, or a volume of some activities, which can be continued only if inflation is also continued, is one of the ways in which even a contemporary inflation places us in a quandary because its discontinuance will necessarily destroy some of the jobs it has created.

But before I turn to those consequences of an economy adjusting itself to a continuous process of inflation, I must deal with an argument that, though I do not know that it has anywhere been clearly stated, seems to lie at the root of the view which represents inflation as relatively harmless. It seems to be that, if future prices are correctly foreseen, any set of prices expected in the future is compatible with an equilibrium position, because present prices will adjust themselves to expected future prices. For this it would, however, clearly not be sufficient that the general level of prices at the various future dates be correctly foreseen, and these, as we have seen, will change in different degrees. The assumption that the future prices of particular commodities can be correctly foreseen during a period of inflation is probably an assumption which never can be true: because, whatever future prices are foreseen, present prices do not by themselves adapt themselves to the expected higher prices of the future, but only through a present increase in the quantity of money with all the changes in the relative height of the different prices which such changes in the quantity of money necessarily involve.

More important, however, is the fact that if future prices were correctly foreseen, inflation would have none of the stimulating effects for which it is welcomed by so many people.

Now the chief effect of inflation which makes it at first generally welcome to business is precisely that prices of products turn out to be higher in general than foreseen. It is this which produces the general state of euphoria, a false sense of wellbeing, in which everybody seems to prosper. Those who without inflation would have made high profits make still higher ones. Those who would have made normal profits make unusually high ones. And not only businesses which were near failure but even some which ought to fail are kept above water by the unexpected boom. There is a general excess of demand over supply—all is saleable and everybody can continue what he had been doing. It is this seemingly blessed state in which there are more jobs than applicants which Lord Beveridge defined as the state of full employment—never understanding that the shrinking value of his pension of which he so bitterly complained in old age was the inevitable consequence of his own recommendations having been followed.

But, and this brings me to my next point, "full employment" in his sense requires not only continued inflation but inflation at a growing rate. Because, as we have seen, it will have its immediate beneficial effect only so long as it, or at least its magnitude, is not foreseen. But once it has continued for some time, its further continuance comes to be expected. If prices have for some time been rising at five percent per annum, it comes to be expected that they will do the same in the future. Present prices of factors are driven up by the expectation of the higher prices for the product—sometimes, where some of the cost elements are fixed, the flexible costs may be driven up even more than the expected rise of the price of the product—up to the point where there will be only a normal profit.

But if prices then do not rise more than expected, no extra profits will be made. Although prices continue to rise at the former rate, this will no longer have the miraculous effect on sales and employment it had before. The artificial gains will disappear, there will again be losses, and some firms will find that prices will not even cover costs. To maintain the effect inflation had earlier when its full extent was not anticipated, it will have to be stronger than before. If at first an annual rate of price increase of five percent had been sufficient, once five percent comes to be expected something like seven percent or more will be necessary to have the same stimulating effect which a five percent rise had before. And since, if inflation has already lasted for some time, a great many activities will have become dependent on its continuance at a progressive rate, we will have a situation in which, in spite of rising prices, many firms will be making losses, and there may be substantial unemployment. Depression with rising prices is a typical consequence of a mere braking of the increase in the rate of inflation once the economy has become geared to a certain rate of inflation.

All this means that, unless we are prepared to accept constantly increasing rates of inflation which in the end would have to exceed any assignable limit, inflation can always give only a temporary fillip to the economy, but must not only cease to have stimulating effect but will always leave us with a legacy of postponed adjustments and new maladjustments which make our problem more difficult. Please note that I am *not* saying that once we embark on inflation we are bound to be drawn into a galloping hyper-inflation. I do not believe that this is true. All I am contending is that *if* we wanted to perpetuate the peculiar prosperity-and-job-creating effects of inflation we would have progressively to step it up and must never stop increasing its rate. That this is so has been empirically confirmed by the Great German inflation of the early 1920s. So long as that increased at a geometrical rate there was indeed (except towards the end) practically no unemployment. But till then every time merely the increase of the rate of inflation slowed down, unemployment rapidly assumed major proportions. I do not believe we shall follow that path—at least not so long as tolerably responsible people are at the helm—though I am not quite so sure that a continuance of the monetary policies of the last decade may not sooner or later create a position in which less responsible people will be put into command. But this is not yet our problem. What we are experiencing is still only what in Britain is known as the "stop-go" policy in which from time to time the authorities get alarmed and try to brake, but only with the result that even before the rise of prices has been brought to a stop, unemployment begins to assume threatening proportions and the authorities feel forced to resume expansion. This sort of thing may go on for quite some time, but I am not sure that the effectiveness of relatively minor doses of inflation in rekindling the boom is not rapidly decreasing. The one thing which, I will admit, has surprised me about the boom of the last twenty years is how long the effectiveness of resumed expansion in restarting the boom has lasted. My expectation was that this power of getting investment under way by a little more credit expansion would much sooner exhaust itself—and it may well be that we have now reached that point. But I am not sure. We may well have another ten years of stop-go policy ahead of us, probably with decreasing effectiveness of the ordinary measures of monetary policy and longer intervals of recessions. Within the political framework and the prevailing state of opinion the present chairman of the Federal Reserve Board will probably do as well as can be expected by anybody. But the limitations imposed upon him by circumstances beyond his control and to which I shall have to turn in a moment may well greatly restrict his ability of doing what we would like to do.

On an earlier occasion on which several of you were present, I have compared the position of those responsible for monetary policy after a full employment policy has been pursued for some time to "holding a tiger by the tail." It seems to me that these two positions have more in common than is comfortable to contemplate. Not only would the tiger tend to run faster and faster and the movement bumpier and bumpier as one is dragged along, but also the prospective effects of letting go become more and more frightening as the tiger becomes more enraged. That one is soon placed in such a position is the central objection against allowing inflation to run on for some time. Another metaphor that has often been justly used in this connection is the effects of drug-taking. The early pleasant effects and the later necessity of a bitter choice constitute indeed a similar dilemma. Once placed in this position it is tempting to rely on palliatives and be content with overcoming short-term difficulties without ever facing the basic trouble about which those solely responsible for monetary policy indeed can do little.

Before I proceed with this main point, however, I must still say a few words about the alleged indispensability of inflation as a condition of rapid growth. We shall see that modern developments of labor union policies in the highly industrialized countries may there indeed have created a position in which both growth and a reasonably high and stable level of employment may, so long as those policies continue, make inflation the only effective means of overcoming the obstacles created by them. But this does not mean that inflation is, in normal conditions, and especially in less developed countries, required or even favorable for growth. None of the great industrial powers of the modern world has reached its position in periods of depreciating money. British prices in 1914 were, so far as meaningful comparisons can be made over such long periods, just about where they had been two hundred years before, and American prices in 1939 were also at about the same level as at the earliest point of time for which we have data, 1749. Though it is largely true that world history is a history of inflation, the few success stories we find are on the whole the stories of countries and periods which have preserved a stable currency; and in the past a deterioration of the value of money has usually gone hand in hand with economic decay.

There is of course, no doubt that temporarily the production of capital goods can be increased by what is called "forced saving"—that is, credit expansion can be used to direct a greater part of the current services of resources to the production of capital goods. At the end of such a period the *physical* quantity of capital goods existing will be greater than it would otherwise have been. Some of this *may* be a lasting gain—people may get houses in return for what they were not allowed to consume. But I am not so sure that such a forced growth of the stock of industrial equipment always makes a country richer, that is, that the *value* of its capital stock will afterwards be greater—or by its assistance all-round productivity be increased more than would otherwise have been the case. If investment was guided by the expectation of a higher rate of continued investment (or a lower rate of interest, or a higher rate of real wages, which all come to the same thing) in the future than in fact will exist, this higher rate of investment may have done less to enhance overall productivity than a lower rate of investment would have done if it had taken more appropriate forms. This I regard as a particularly serious danger for underdeveloped countries that rely on inflation to step up the rate of investment. The regular effect of this seems to me to be that a small fraction of the workers of such countries is equipped with an amount of capital per head much larger than it can hope within the foreseeable future to provide for all its workers, and that the investment of the larger total in consequence does less to raise the general standard of living than a smaller total more widely and evenly spread would have done. Those who counsel underdeveloped countries to speed up the rate of growth by inflation seem to me wholly irresponsible to an almost criminal degree. The one condition which, on Keynesian assumptions, makes inflation necessary to secure a full utilization of resources, namely the rigidity of wage rates determined by labor unions, is not present there. And nothing I have seen of the effects of such policies, be it in South America, Africa, or Asia, can change my conviction that in such countries inflation is entirely and exclusively damaging—producing a waste of resources and delaying the development of that spirit of rational calculation which is the indispensable condition of the growth of an efficient market economy.

The whole Keynesian argument for an expansionist credit policy rests entirely and completely on the existence of that union determined level of money wages which is characteristic of the industrially advanced countries of the West but is absent in underdeveloped countries—and for different reasons less marked in countries like Japan and Germany. It is only for those countries where, as it is said, money wages are "rigid downward" and are constantly pushed up by union pressure that a plausible case can be made that a high level of employment can be maintained only by continuous inflation—and I have no doubt that we will get this so long as those conditions persist. What has happened here at the end of the last war has been that principles of policy have been adopted, and often embodied in the law, which in effect release unions of all responsibility for the unemployment their wage policies may cause and place all responsibility for the preservation of full employment on the monetary and fiscal authorities. The latter are in effect required to provide enough money so that the supply of labor at the wages fixed by the unions can be taken off the market. And since it cannot be denied that at least for a period of years the monetary authorities have the power by sufficient inflation to secure a high level of employment, they will be forced by public opinion to use that instrument. This is the sole cause of the inflationary developments of the last twenty-five years, and it will continue to operate as long as we allow on the one hand the unions to drive up money wages to whatever level they can get employers to consent to—and these employers consent to money wages with a present buying power which they can accept only because they know the monetary authorities will partly undo the harm by lowering the purchasing power of money and thereby also the real equivalent of the agreed money wages.

This is the political fact which for the present makes continued inflation inevitable and which can be altered not by any changes in monetary but only by changes in wage policy. Nobody should have any illusion about the fact that so long as the present position on the labor market lasts we are bound to have continued inflation. Yet we cannot afford this, not only because inflation becomes less and less effective even in preventing unemployment, but because after it has lasted for some time and comes to operate at a high rate, it begins progressively to disorganize the economy and to create strong pressure for the imposition of all kinds of controls. Open inflation is bad enough, but inflation repressed by controls is even worse: it is the real end of the market economy.

The hot iron which we must grasp if we are to preserve the enterprise system and the free market is, therefore, the power of the unions over wages. Unless wages, and particularly the relative wages in the different industries, are again subjected to the forces of the market and become truly flexible, in particular groups downwards as well as upwards, there is no possibility for a non-inflationary policy. A very simple consideration shows that, if no wage is allowed to fall, all the changes in relative wages which become necessary must be brought about by all the wages except those who tend to fall relatively most being adjusted upwards. This means that practically all money wages must rise if any change in the wage structure is to be brought about. Yet a labor union conceding a reduction of the wages of its members appears today to be an impossibility. Nobody, of course, gains from this situation, since the rise in money wages must be offset by a depreciation of the value of money if no unemployment is to be caused. It seems, however, a built-in necessity of that determination of wages by collective bargaining by industrial or craft unions plus a full employment policy.

I believe that so long as this fundamental issue is not resolved, there is little to be hoped from any improvement of the machinery of monetary control. But this does not mean that the existing arrangements are satisfactory. They have been designed precisely to make it easier to give in to the necessities determined by the wage problem, i.e., to make it easier for each country to inflate. The gold standard has been destroyed chiefly because it was an obstacle to inflation. When in 1931 a few days after the suspension of the gold standard in Great Britain Lord Keynes wrote in a London newspaper that "there are few Englishmen who do not rejoice at the breaking of our gold fetters," and fifteen years later could assure us that Bretton Woods arrangements were "the opposite of the gold standard," all this was directed against the very feature of the gold standard by which it made impossible any prolonged inflationary policy of any one country. And though I am not sure that the gold standard is the best conceivable arrangement for that purpose, it has been the only one that has been fairly successful in doing so. It probably has many defects, but the reason for which it has been destroyed was not one of them; and what has been put into its place is no improvement. If, as I have recently heard it explained by one of the members of the original Bretton Woods group, their aim was to place the burden of adjustment of international balances exclusively on the surplus countries, it seems to me the result of this must be continued international inflation. But I only mention this in conclusion to show that if we are to avoid continued world-wide inflation, we need also a different international monetary system. Yet the time when we can profitably think about this will be only after the leading countries have solved their internal problems. Till then we probably have to be satisfied with makeshifts, and it seems to me that at the present time, and so long as the fundamental difficulties I have considered continue to be present, there is no chance of meeting the problem of international inflation by restoring an international gold standard, even if this were practical policy. The central problem which must be solved before we can hope for a satisfactory monetary order is the problem of wage determination.

The Austrian Theory: A Summary

Roger W. Garrison

Grounded in the economic theory set out in Carl Menger's *Principles of Economics* and built on the vision of a capital-using production process developed in Eugen von Böhm-Bawerk's *Capital and Interest*, the Austrian theory of the business cycle remains sufficiently distinct to justify its national identification. But even in its earliest rendition in Ludwig von Mises's *Theory of Money and Credit* and in subsequent exposition and extension in F. A. Hayek's *Prices and Production*, the theory incorporated important elements from Swedish and British economics. Knut Wicksell's *Interest and Prices*, which showed how prices respond to a discrepancy between the bank rate and the real rate of interest, provided the basis for the Austrian account of the misallocation of capital during the boom. The market process that eventually reveals the intertemporal misallocation and turns boom into bust resembles an analogous

This "Summary" is adapted from Roger W. Garrison, "The Austrian Theory of the Business Cycle," in David Glasner, ed., *Business Cycles and Depressions: An Encyclopedia* (New York:Garland Publishing, 1996).

process described by the British Currency School, in which international misallocations induced by credit expansion are subsequently eliminated by changes in the terms of trade and hence in specie flow.

The Austrian theory of the business cycle emerges straight-forwardly from a simple comparison of savings-induced growth, which is sustainable, with a credit-induced boom, which is not. An increase in saving by individuals and a credit expansion orchestrated by the central bank set into motion market processes whose initial allocational effects on the economy's capital structure are similar. But the ultimate consequences of the two processes stand in stark contrast: Saving gets us genuine growth; credit expansion gets us boom and bust.

The general thrust of the theory, though not the full argument, can be stated in terms of the conventional macroeconomic aggregates of saving and investment. The level of investment is determined by the supply of and demand for loanable funds, as shown in Figures 1a and 1b. Supply reflects the willingness of individuals to save at various rates of interest; demand reflects the willingness of businesses to borrow and undertake investment projects. Each figure represents a state of equilibrium in the loan market: the market-clearing rate of interest is i, as shown on the vertical axis; the amount of income saved and borrowed for investment purposes is A, as shown on the horizontal axis.

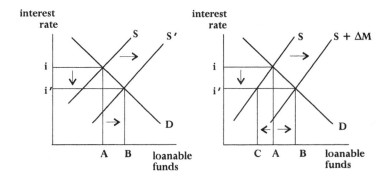

Figure 1a   Figure 1b

An increase in the supply of loanable funds, as shown in both figures, has obvious initial effects on the interest rate and on the level of investment borrowing. But the market process plays itself out differently depending upon whether the increased supply of loanable funds derives from increased saving by individuals or from increased credit creation by the central bank.

Figure 1a shows the market's reaction to an increase in the thriftiness of individuals, as represented by a shift of the supply curve from S to S '. People have become more future-oriented; they prefer to shift consumption from the present to the future. As a result of the increased availability of loanable funds, the rate of interest falls from i to i ', enticing businesses to undertake investment projects previously considered unprofitable. At the new lower market-clearing rate of interest, both saving and investment increase by the amount AB. This increase in the economy's productive capacity constitutes genuine growth.

Figure 1b shows the effect of an increase in credit creation brought about by the central bank, as represented by a shift of the supply curve from S to $S + \Delta M$. Here it is assumed that people have *not* become more thrifty or future-oriented; the central bank has simply inflated the supply of loanable funds by injecting new money into credit markets. As the market-clearing rate of interest falls from i to i ', businesses are enticed to increase investment by the amount AB, while genuine saving actually falls by the amount AC. Padding the supply of loanable funds with newly created money holds the interest rate artificially low and drives a wedge between saving and investment. The low bank rate of interest has stimulated growth in the absence of any new saving. The credit-induced artificial boom is inherently unsustainable and is followed inevitably by a bust, as investment falls back into line with saving.

Even in this simple loanable-funds framework, many aspects of the Austrian theory of the business cycle are evident. The natural rate of interest is the rate that equates saving and investment. The bank rate diverges from the natural rate as a result of credit expansion. When new money is injected into credit markets, the injection effects, which the Austrian theorists emphasize over price-level effects, take the form of too much investment. And actual investment in excess of desired saving, CB, constitutes what Austrian theorists call forced saving.

Other significant aspects of the Austrian theory of the business cycle can be identified only after the simple concept of investment represented in Figures 1a and 1b is replaced by the Austrian vision of a multistage, time-consuming production process. The rate of interest governs not only the level of investment but also the allocation of resources *within* the investment sector. The economy's intertemporal structure of production consists of investment subaggregates, which are defined in terms of their temporal relationship to the consumer goods they help to produce. Some stages of production, such as research and development and resource extraction, are temporally distant from the output of consumer goods. Other stages, such as wholesale and retail operations, are temporally close to final goods in the hands of consumers. As implied by standard calculations of discounted factor values, interest-rate sensitivity increases with the temporal distance of the investment subaggregate, or stage of production, from final consumption.

The interest rate governs the intertemporal pattern of resource allocation. For an economy to exhibit equilibrating tendencies over time, the intertemporal pattern of resource allocation must adjust to changes in the intertemporal pattern of consumption preferences. An increase in the rate of saving implies a change in the preferred consumption pattern such that planned consumption is shifted from the near future to the remote future. A savings-induced decrease in the rate of interest favors investment over current consumption, as shown in Figures 1a and 1b. Further—and more significant in Austrian theorizing—it favors investment in more durable over less durable capital and in capital suited for temporally more remote rather than less remote stages of production. These are the kinds of changes within the capital structure that are necessary to shift output from the near future to the more remote future in conformity with changing intertemporal consumption preferences.

The shift of capital away from final output—and hence the shift of output towards the more remote future—can also be induced by credit creation. However, the credit-induced decrease in the rate of interest engenders a *dis*conformity between intertemporal resource usage and intertemporal consumption preferences. Market mechanisms that allocate resources within the capital structure are imperfect enough to permit substantial intertemporal disequilibria, but the market process that shifts output from the near to the more remote future when savings preferences have not changed is bound to be ill-fated. The spending pattern of income earners clashes with the production decisions that generated their income. The intertemporal mismatch between earning and spending patterns eventually turns boom into bust. More specifically, the artificially low rate of interest that triggered the boom eventually gives way to a high real rate of interest as overcommitted investors bid against one another for increasingly scarce resources. The bust, which is simply the market's recognition of the unsustainability of the boom, is followed by liquidation and capital restructuring through which production activities are brought back into conformity with consumption preferences.

Mainstream macroeconomics bypasses all issues involving intertemporal capital structure by positing a simple inverse relationship between aggregate (net) investment and the interest rate. The investment aggregate is typically taken to be interest-inelastic in the context of short-run macroeconomic theory and policy prescription and interest-elastic in the context of long-run growth. Further, the very simplicity of this formulation suggests that expectations—which are formulated in the light of current and anticipated policy prescriptions—can make or break policy effectiveness. The Austrian theory recognizes that whatever the interest elasticity of the conventionally defined investment aggregate, the impact of interest-rate movements on the structure of capital is crucial to the maintenance of intertemporal equilibrium. Changes within the capital structure may be significant even when the change in net investment is not. And those structural changes can be equilibrating or disequilibrating depending on whether they are savings-induced or credit-induced, or—more generally—depending on whether they are preference-induced or policy-induced. Further, the very complexity of the interplay between preferences and policy within a multistage intertemporal capital structure suggests that market participants cannot fully sort out and hedge against the effects of policy on product and factor prices.

In mainstream theory, a change in the conventionally defined investment aggregate not accommodated by an increase in saving, commonly identified as *over*investment and represented as CB in Figure 1b, is often downplayed on both theoretical and empirical grounds. In Austrian theory, the possibility of overinvestment is recognized, but the central concern is with the more complex and insidious *mal*investment (not represented at all in Figure 1b) which involves the intertemporal misallocation of resources within the capital structure.

Conventionally, business cycles are marked by changes in employment and in total output. The Austrian theory suggests that the boom and bust are more meaningfully identified with intertemporal misallocations of resources within the economy's capital structure followed by liquidation and capital restructuring. Under extreme assumptions about labor mobility, an economy could undergo policy-induced intertemporal misallocations and the subsequent reallocation with no change in total employment. Actual market processes, however, involve adjustments in both capital and labor markets that translate capital-market misallocations into labor-market fluctuations. During the artificial boom, when workers are bid away from late stages of production into earlier stages, unemployment is low; when the boom ends, workers are simply released from failing businesses, and their absorption into new or surviving firms is time-consuming.

Mainstream theory distinguishes between broadly conceived structural unemployment (a mismatch of job openings and job applicants) and cyclical unemployment (a decrease in job openings). In the Austrian view, cyclical unemployment is, at least initially, a particular kind of structural unemployment: the credit-induced restructuring of capital has created too many jobs in the early stages of production. A relatively high level of unemployment ushered in by the bust involves workers whose subsequent employment prospects depend on reversing the credit-induced capital restructuring.

The Austrian theory allows for the possibility that while malinvested capital is being liquidated and reabsorbed elsewhere in the economy's intertemporal capital structure, unemployment can increase dramatically as reduced incomes and reduced spending feed upon one another. The self-aggravating contraction of economic activity was designated as a "secondary depression" by the Austrians to distinguish it from the structural maladjustment that, in their view, is the primary problem. By contrast, mainstream theories, particularly Keynesianism, which ignore the intertemporal capital structure, deal exclusively with the downward spiral.

Questions of policy and institutional reform are answered differently by Austrian and mainstream economists because of the difference in focus as between intertemporal misallocations and downward spirals. The Austrians, who see the intertemporal distortion of the capital structure as the more fundamental problem, recommend monetary reform aimed at avoiding credit-induced booms. Hard money and decentralized banking are key elements of the Austrian reform agenda. Mainstream macroeconomists take structural problems (intertemporal or otherwise) to be completely separate from the general problem of demand deficiency and the periodic problem of downward spirals of demand and income. Their policy prescriptions, which include fiscal and monetary stimulants aimed at maintaining economic expansion, are seen by the Austrians as the primary source of intertemporal distortions of the capital structure.

Although the purging in the 1930s of capital theory from macroeconomics consigned the Austrian theory of the business cycle to a minority view, a number of economists working within the Austrian tradition continue the development of capital-based macroeconomics.

Further Reading

Bellante, Don and Roger W. Garrison. "Phillips Curves and Hayekian Triangles: Two Perspectives on Monetary Dynamics," *History of Political Economy* 20, no. 2 (Summer 1988): 207–34.

Butos, William N. "The Recession and Austrian Business Cycle Theory: An Empirical Perspective," *Critical Review* 7, nos. 2–3 (Spring–Winter 1993): 277–306.

Garrison, Roger W. "Austrian Capital Theory and the Future of Macroeconomics," in Richard M. Ebeling, ed. *Austrian Economics: Perspectives on the Past and Prospects for the Future* (Hillsdale, Mich.: Hillsdale College Press, 1991), pp. 303–24.

——. "The Austrian Theory of the Business Cycle in the Light of Modern Macroeconomics," *Review of Austrian Economics* 3 (1989): 3–29.

——. "The Hayekian Trade Cycle Theory: A Reappraisal," *Cato Journal* 6, no. 2 (Fall 1986): 437–53.

——. "Time and Money: The Universals of Macroeconomic Theorizing," *Journal of Macroeconomics* 6, no. 2 (Spring 1984): 197–213.

O'Driscoll, Gerald P., Jr. *Economics as a Coordination Problem: The Contribution of Friedrich A. Hayek* (Kansas City: Sheed Andrews and McMeel, 1977).

Rothbard, Murray N. *The Case Against the Fed* (Auburn, Ala.: Ludwig von Mises Institute, 1995).

Skousen, Mark. *The Structure of Production* (New York: New York University Press, 1990).

Wainhouse, Charles E. "Empirical Evidence for Hayek's Theory of Economic Fluctuations," in Barry N. Siegel, ed., *Money in Crises: The Federal Reserve, the Economy, and Monetary Reform* (Cambridge, Mass.: Ballinger Publishing, 1984), pp. 37–66.

Index

(Prepared by Timothy Terrell)

Beveridge, Lord William, 100
Böhm-Bawerk, Eugen von, 9, 27, 111
Bretton Woods, 109, 110
Business cycle
    Austrian theory of, 7–10, 17–21,
        25–35, 27n, 37–64, 81–91,
        111–20
    Currency school theory of
    See Currency school, British
    Keynesian theory of, 21, 22, 66,
        67, 120
    Marxist theory of, 69
    monetarist theory of, 22–23
    Ricardian theory of, 74–81

Cantillon, Richard, 97
Capital
    accumulation, 51, 105
    in Austrian macroeconomics, 17,
        18, 111, 120
    circulating, 10, 11, 51
    confiscation through taxation, 95
    fixed, 10, 51, 62, 63
    and Hayekian triangles, 10
    intertemporal structure of, 11, 13,
        14, 116–20
    See also time dimension
    in mainstream macroeconomics,
        12, 18, 117, 120
    misallocation of, 9, 14, 21, 30, 50,
        54, 61, 83–86, 105, 111,
        116–20
    restructuring following boom, 14,
        73, 84, 117–119
    in underdeveloped countries, 106
    See also production
Cassel, Gustav, 44
Central bank, 13, 20, 21, 28, 30–35,

42–45, 78–81, 93, 107, 108,
112–14
    See also Federal Reserve System
Communism, 53–54
Coolidge, Calvin, 88–89
    Currency school, British, 8, 9,
        25–27, 112

Deflation, 11, 16, 44, 48, 58-61
Depression
    as a period of adjustment, 53, 61,
        62, 77, 80, 84–87
    definition of, 65–66
    following credit expansion, 30, 34,
        45, 57, 77, 86–87
    and gold production, 48, 58–60
    Great Depression, 16, 32, 39, 48,
        59, 65, 88–90
    Keynesian psychological explana-
        tion of, 12
    length and depth of, 14, 34, 89
    price level during, 40, 46–48, 77, 101
    prolonged by wage and price
        rigidity, 33, 47, 87–89
    Salerno–Tullock exchange, 17, 18
    secondary, 15, 18, 58, 119
    theory of, 8, 72–74, 90
    volume of payments during, 41
    See also business cycle

Entrepreneurship, 7, 71, 72, 80, 86
Expectations, 7, 23, 99–101, 105, 117

Federal Reserve System, 79, 88–89, 103
Fisher, Irving, 11, 46
Forced saving, 56, 105, 115
    See also capital, misallocation of

Friedman, Milton, 22

Garrison, Roger W., 7, 111
General Theory of Employment, Interest,
    and Money
    See Keynes, John Maynard
Gold
    production of, 48, 60
    standard, 25, 26, 28, 32, 59– 60,
        88, 90, 109–10, 120
Great Depression
    See depression

Haberler, Gottfried, 7, 10, 11, 14–16, 37
Hansen, Alvin, 90
Hawtrey, Ralph, 44–47, 61
Hayek, Friedrich A. von
    and central bank policy, 20
    and the Hayekian triangle
    See under capital
    vs. Keynesianism, 12, 13
    Monetary Theory and the Trade Cycle,
        81
    Prices and Production, 58, 81, 111
    as a proponent of Austrian busi-
        ness cycle theory, 80, 90
Hayekian triangles
    See capital
Hicks, John R., 17, 96n
Hoover, Herbert, 89
Hume, David, 74, 97
Hyperinflation, 19, 20, 102
    in interwar Germany, 19, 30, 32, 102

Industrial Revolution, 69
Inflation
    causes of, 20, 44, 45, 66, 75, 79,
        107–10
    effects of, 29–32, 59–60, 63–64,
        73, 76–77, 80, 84–86,
        94–106, 108
    See hyperinflation
    and overspending in Keynesian

analysis, 66–68
    premium, 11
    solutions to, 86–88, 93, 108–10
    squelched in a competitive bank-
        ing industry, 78
    with no increase in commodity
        prices, 48, 49
Interest rate
    and allocation of resources, 9, 11,
        13, 28–30, 52–53, 62–63,
        83–84, 106, 115–17
    See also capital, misallocation of
    artificial, 9, 21, 32, 111, 114, 117
    manipulation of, 28, 30–31,
        34–35, 45, 81–82, 85, 114
    natural, or real, 8, 11, 13, 81–82,
        111–14, 117

Kaldor, Nicholas, 17
Keynesianism, 12, 13, 21–23, 66, 88,
    90–91, 106–7, 120
    Keynesian revolution, 8, 90
Keynes, John Maynard
    and "capital-free" macroeconom-
        ics, 12–13
    and the destruction of the gold
        standard, 109
    General Theory of Employment, Inter-
        est, and Money, 8, 66, 90
    and government intervention in
        the economy, 66–67
    and the misallocation of capital
        through credit inflation,
        62–63
    See also Keynesianism and business
        cycle, Keynesian theory of

Laissez-faire policy, 88, 90
Lerner, Abba P., 17

McCracken, Paul W., 67–68
Marx, Karl, 69
Menger, Carl, 9, 27, 111
    Principles of Economics, 111

Mises, Ludwig von
  on the acceptance of Austrian business cycle theory, 7
  on business cycles, 9, 19, 20, 25, 81–86, 96
  on government intervention during economic crises, 86–88
  on Lionel Robbins, 15
  on the Great Depression, 89, 90
  on real interest rates, 11
  Theory of Money and Credit, 8, 80, 111
Monetarism, 13, 22–23

New Deal, 89
Nixon, Richard, 67

Peel's Bank Act of 1844, 26
Phillips curve, 13
Prices
  of commodities, 30, 48
  of consumer goods, 56
  general level of, 9, 11, 45–47, 49, 60, 80, 96–99, 105
  international variations in level of, 26, 76–77
  of producer goods, 56, 84–85, 87
  relative, 11, 85, 96–98
  stabilization of, 43, 46, 63, 87, 89
  See also deflation; inflation; wage-price spiral
Price theory, 70–71
Production
  horizontal structure of, 50
  process distortion, 9, 11, 19, 28–29, 46–63, 83–85, 98, 105, 116
  roundaboutness of, 10–11, 19, 52–54, 57, 63, 83, 115
  time element in, 13, 20, 53, 57, 83, 115–16
  See also time dimension
  vertical structure of, 11, 14, 49–53

Recession, 66–67, 72, 87, 103

  See also business cycle; depression
Ricardo, David, 74
Robbins, Lionel
  recantation of Austrian theory, 15, 16
  The Great Depression, 15, 28n
Robertson, Dennis, 57
Roosevelt, Franklin Delano, 89
Rothbard, Murray N., 8, 12–13, 17, 24, 65
Roundaboutness
  See under production

Salerno, Joseph T., 17, 18
Socialism, 68

Theory of Money and Credit
  See Mises, Ludwig von
Time dimension, 10, 13, 18–19, 23, 115
  See also production, time element in
Time preference, 81–82, 84, 113–14, 116–17
Trade cycle
  See business cycle
Tullock, Gordon, 17, 18

Unemployment, 13–14, 18, 67–68, 87, 89, 101–3, 107–9, 119
Unions, 20, 33, 104, 106–9

Wage-price spiral, 13, 20, 28–29
Wages
  governmental manipulation of, 20, 87, 89, 108
  increasing as a result of credit inflation, 28–29, 56, 83
  rigidity of, 33, 35, 47, 106–9
  union manipulation of, 20, 33, 106-9
  See also wage-price spiral
Wicksell, Knut 8, 9, 27
  Interest and Prices, 111
Wieser, Friedrich von, 27

Ludwig von Mises (1881–1973), leading proponent of the Austrian School in the 20th century, received his doctorate from the University of Vienna, where he taught. He was also economic advisor to the Austrian Chamber of Commerce. Mises later taught at the Graduate Institute for International Studies in Geneva and New York University. His most important works include *The Theory of Money and Credit*, *Socialism*, *Theory and History*, and *Human Action*.

Gottfried Haberler (1900–1995) received his doctorate from the University of Vienna, and taught there as well as at Harvard University. A student of Mises's, he was also resident scholar at the American Enterprise Institute and a distinguished scholar of the Ludwig von Mises Institute. His most important works include *The Sense of Index Numbers*, *Theory of International Trade*, *Prosperity and Depression*, and *Economic Growth and Stability*.

Murray N. Rothbard (1926–1995) received his doctorate from Columbia University. He also studied with Mises at New York University. He taught at New York Polytechnic Institute and the University of Nevada, Las Vegas, where he held the S.J. Hall Chair. He was also academic vice president of the Ludwig von Mises Institute from its founding. His most important works include *Man, Economy, and State*, *Power and Market*, *America's Great Depression*, and *The History of Economic Thought*.

Friedrich A. Hayek (1899–1992) received his doctorate from the University of Vienna, and taught there as well as at the London School of Economics, the University of Chicago, and the University of Freiburg. A student of Mises's and the recipient of the Nobel Prize in Economics for his work with Mises, Hayek was a distinguished scholar of the Ludwig von Mises Institute. His most important works include *Prices and Production*, *Monetary Theory and the Trade Cycle*, *Monetary Nationalism and International Stability*, and *The Pure Theory of Capital*.

* * * * *

Roger W. Garrison received his doctorate from the University of Virginia and is Professor of Economics at Auburn University. He lectures for the Ludwig von Mises Institute and directs its Austrian Economics Workshop. He is also the author of many important articles on macroeconomics, and is considered a leading business-cycle theorist in the Austrian School.